CONCILIUM

Religion in the Eighties

CONCILIUM

General Secretariat: Prins Bernhardstraat 2, 6521 AB Nijmegen, The Netherlands
Concilium 186 (4/1986): Practical Theology

CONCILIUM

List of Members

Advisory Committee: Practical Theology

POPULAR RELIGION

Edited by
Norbert Greinacher

and
Norbert Mette

English Language Editor
Marcus Lefébure

T. & T. CLARK LTD
Edinburgh

August 1986
T. & T. Clark Ltd, 59 George Street, Edinburgh EH2 2LQ
ISBN: 0 567 30066 8

ISSN: 0010-5236

Typeset by Print Origination Formby Liverpool
Printed by Page Brothers (Norwich) Ltd

Concilium: Published February, April, June, August, October, December.
Subscriptions 1986: UK: £19.95 (including postage and packing); USA: US$40.00
(including air mail postage and packing); Canada: Canadian $50.00 (including air mail
postage and packing); other countries; £19.95 (including postage and packing).

CONTENTS

vii

Part II
Theological Perspectives on Popular Religion

Part III
Popular Religion as a Challenge to Church Practice

EDITORIAL

CONCILIUM HAS already discussed the topic of 'popular religion' or 'folk religion' in a series of articles. Furthermore, two issues have been devoted to the concept and meaning of the 'people' in the Church and in theology.[1] The present issue is a further contribution to this discussion.

For a long time the view governing both theological reflection and pastoral practice was that 'popular religion' consisted of vestiges of superstition and religious ignorance which had somehow not been 'christianised'. In more recent times, however, this view has been replaced by a productive re-evaluation which has even found its way into official Church documents,[2] namely, that faith is expressed in popular religion in a form that is historically concrete, social and cultural. Its substance and practices simply and directly express people's fundamental concerns, such as the meaning of life, of suffering, and of an after-life. Thus popular religion helps to give coherence and a sense of direction to life; it is a central factor in creating and maintaining individual and collective identity. Without being thematised in reflective thought, rooted in specific ways in the life of the people, it constitutes a particular expression of discipleship. To that extent it can rightly be said to be a potential source of evangelism (see Puebla 450).

However, the religious life of the people, subject as it is to socio-historical conditions, is always ambivalent and so stands in need of the liberation which the Gospel brings. Precisely because man's religious practice touches the deepest layers of individual and collective identity, its misuse opens up the most profound possibilities of alienation and oppression; it can hold people in the grip of irreversible regression; it can have pathological and destructive effects.

ix

The present issue aims to guide the reader to act in a theologically responsible way, on the one hand bearing in mind the potential ambivalence of popular piety, and on the other bringing out its creative impulses. Since it is determined by its particular socio-cultural matrix, popular piety will present a multiplicity of forms and approaches. The present issue of *Concilium* hopes to do justice to this fact by devoting the *first part* of this issue—after the survey attempted by L. Maldonado—to case studies from various countries, illustrating and analysing different expressions of popular religion. This spectrum makes it very clear how strongly the religious life of a people or a group is influenced by the components of a counter-culture when it comes to putting forward a model of 'true life'—whether in contrast to an 'officially' administered religion, or in resistance to cultural and political alienation and oppression. Unsatisfied longings and hopes for fulfilment also find expression here, though they are often put merely in terms of 'waiting for other-worldly consolations',[3] or are deliberately channelled in that direction.

The articles in parts two and three also contain concrete illustrations. This accords with the fact that instances of popular religion, in terms of living out the Gospel, can only be judged 'on their merits'. In order to allow the liberating potential of popular religion to come into play, it is necessary to expose and point out the various mechanisms of oppression, in Church and society, which have penetrated it, and critically to distinguish the various ways of dealing with it. The articles in this issue have made a start in demonstrating how particular, dominant social forms (as well as Church forms), necessarily bring about, by way of reaction, very particular modes of popular religion or their equivalents (as one ought to say in connection with many manifestations in the so-called 'secularised' societies). Historical studies are indispensable if we are to understand the processes of transformation thus involved in popular religion. J. Delumeau gives an instructive example of this; but brief references to the relevant historical contexts are also to be found in other contributions.

All the time, however, we must be aware that theological and theoretical reflection is always in danger of subjecting popular piety to a constricting system. In this issue of *Concilium* we have tried to counteract this tendency somewhat by giving space to diverse approaches and positions. It will be seen that contributions from, and about, Latin America predominate; this reflects the fact that discussion and clarification of popular religion is being carried on most intensively in that subcontinent.[4]

Following the case studies, the articles in *part two* present for discussion various theological theses and hypotheses on the significance of popular religion and the criteria for evaluating it. There is a wide spectrum of approaches to it, ranging from toleration and 'official' monopolisation, to outright opposition; this is not a new phenomenon, as H. Vorländer shows us in his remarks on the Old Testament. The contributions of E. Henau and E. Dussel differ considerably from one another due to their different backgrounds and theological contexts, yet their respective emphases are not opposed. It emerges that it is important, in attaining clarification and evaluation, to see just what is meant by speaking of the 'people' as the carrier of religiosity, and also to understand the reciprocal relationship of religiosity and faith.

Concrete examples again play a big part in the contributions to *part three*, which deals with the challenge to ecclesial practice represented by popular religion. Here all agree that there can be no question of 'using' popular religion as an instrument for some other end; it can only be recognised as authentic. It must not be regulated 'from above'; rather, individuals and groups must be allowed to cultivate appropriate forms of expression for their faith. We have a permanent obligation to plead for the rights of an authentic popular religion. Otherwise we shall be merely paying lip-service to the much-vaunted 'inculturation' of the faith.

Translated by Graham Harrison   Norbert Greinacher
                                                  Norbert Mette

Notes

1. *Concilium* 176 (6/ 1984) 'La Iglesia Popular: Between Fear and Hope'; *Concilium* 180 (4/ 1985) 'The Teaching Authority of the Believers'.
2. See especially EN 48; Puebla 444–468.
3. P.M. Zulehner *Leutereligion* (Vienna 1982) p. 15.
4. H. Ribeiro *Religiosidada popular na teologia latinoamericana* (Sao Paulo 1984) has an ample bibliography.

Part I

Popular Religion in the Cultural Context

Luis Maldonado

Popular Religion: Its Dimensions, Levels and Types

THE INTEREST in popular religion, within both the Catholic Church in general and pastoral theology in particular, was aroused by the meeting of the CELAM in Medellın in 1968, and consolidated by that at Puebla ten years later.

The new movement's concrete origin has also influenced its approach. In effect Medellín was concerned with popular religion for two reasons: first, that it was *reacting against an élitist approach* to pastoral practice, and secondly, that it was counteracting a pastoral practice characterised by a *very European, particularly central-European, culture.*[1]

The élitist approach resulted from the excessive influence of such specialised movements of Catholic Action as Jec, Joc, etc., which basically centred on the so-called teams of militants (never more than a few persons). It also arose from the way in which liturgical reform was developing—that is to say, through very 'select' groups, of rather refined, aesthetically-inclined culture, completely bourgeois, middle-class, not at all 'of the people'.

Opening the way for popular religion is, therefore, in essence, an invitation to a *pastoral practice for the masses.* More than that, it is a powerful recall to the vocation and desire which the Church has had and repeatedly demonstrated in the course of the twenty centuries of its history, namely to be a Church for the masses, and never to succumb to the temptation to allow itself to be reduced to a mere sect.[2]

3

Popular religion is where the masses are. That is where the vast majority of the population are to be found, at least in countries belonging to the Catholic tradition.

In the Latin-American Church, certainly, the movement is biased towards the multitude, along with the Basic Community movement, which forms a link between the masses and the little team of militants, and which serves as an organ of critical awareness and of spiritual and prophetic inspiration, capable of bringing to life and evangelising the rather ponderous body of popular religion.

From another angle, since Medellín (and also since *Gaudium et Spes*), there has been an explicit quest for a synthesis between the faith and indigenous cultures—that is, the great task of *inculturation*. And popular religion is precisely a vast, colossal example of a by no means negative syncretisation between the Gospel and peoples' own cultures, their own creations, heritages, and pre-Christian legacies.[3]

Is the phenomenon of any interest at the present time outside Latin America? We have to recognise a paradoxical fact. In some places it could be said that popular religion has almost disappeared or has been repressed, marginalised or distorted by its environmental context, so that it has degenerated into superstition, sorcery, astrology, etc. Thus in some developed countries, and in large cities, great movements of population, secularisation and the technical-pragmatic mentality have caused it almost to disappear.

By contrast, in other places (not always underdeveloped) popular religion is enjoying a boom, or is at least holding its own and maintaining a surprising attraction, even for young people. Numerous examples could be quoted from Spanish- and Portuguese- speaking areas, both in the Iberian Peninsula and in Latin America. So far as places of pilgrimage are concerned, in Europe as well as elsewhere, there is a definite increase in the number of visitors.

It may be said that all this is no more than a resurgence of interest in religion resulting from the current crisis-situation, and a belief that the end of the world is near.

It is precisely this kind of reductionist conclusion ('it is only that . . . ') that current theological-pastoral reflection, now carried out on an inter-disciplinary basis (ethnological, anthropological, etc.), seeks to avoid. For it becomes increasingly clear from such reflection that popular religion is an *extremely complex reality*, comprising a multiplicity of elements. The same could be said of the concept or category of 'people'.

In fact when we try to explain who or what is the subject of this 'popular' religion—that is to say, the *people*—we find that there are *two lines of interpretation*, both of which deserve to be taken into account.

It was Medellín which first understood the word 'people' to mean the poor people, the mass of peasants or marginalised urban workers, suffering a whole range of deprivations. It is the opposite of a minority, in both a quantitative and a qualitative sense.

But there is also the view held by other bishops and theologians in Latin American—notably the Argentinians—who already some years previously had interpreted 'people' in a different way. The word is taken to mean not a section, a sub-group or a fraction, but a totality. By 'people' they mean the people of the nation—in the case in point, the Argentinian people. According to them, the concept of 'people' has three constitutive elements: a collective subject, a common culture, and a common history.[4]

The documents from Puebla (i.e. from the Third Conference of Latin American bishops in February 1979) try to hold together the two meanings which the word 'people' had acquired through the studies of previous years.[5]

Contemporary sociology also has this tendency to be not exclusive but conciliatory, and tries to hold together and even to give expression to both concepts of 'people'.[6] The starting-point for this exercise is a very elementary and primary linguistic fact. In many dictionaries of present-day Western languages, the word 'people' always has two distinct meanings. According to the first, 'people' refers to the totality of the people who belong to the same country and live under the same laws. They may hold in common the same origin, the same religion, language, culture. In the second sense, 'people' is that part of the nation or of the population which considers itself to be in opposition to the classes which are better off, have more education and more power.

To sum up, it is clear that we must not deny the unity expressed by the global concept of 'people'. But neither can we ignore its divisions, the splits which appear in it precisely because of the confrontations and separations which it contains, and which have their origin in unjust economic systems of ownership, production and distribution of resources. It is also clear that these two ways of understanding 'people' must be reflected in popular culture and piety, since these are the multiform expression of the plural reality of the people. But, as V. Lanternari says: 'Popular religion in all its manifestations cannot be adequately understood in terms of class. The demarcation line between popular and official religion passes through factors of ethnic and cultural identity, as well as through factors of class. There is no such thing as a single, unchanging popular religion. There are different popular religions, as the title of the First International Colloquy held in Quebec in 1970 declares. Popular religion varies to the extent that historico-cultural circumstances vary.'[7]

When we turn to what can be understood as 'religion' in this popular context, some interesting lines of enquiry are suggested by this same Quebec Colloquy. The main paper was delivered by M. Meslin, Professor of the History of Religions at the Sorbonne.[8] His conclusions may be summarised as follows:

Popular religion is the quest for (a) *more simple*, (b) *more direct*, and (c) *more profitable relationships with the divine.*

The quest for 'more simple relationships' means the attempt to get away from an over-intellectualised, over-conceptualised, cerebral, abstract, 'dogmatic' form of religious practice. It is a quest for more intuitive, more imaginative forms, in which the feeling and the imaginative force of the people can be fully developed and expressed.

The quest for 'more direct relationships' means the rejection of clerical and clericalistic mediation between man and the divinity. Such mediation is seen more as an obstacle or oppressive wall than as communication and service.

As can be seen, these first two aspects are, or can be, in themselves, perfectly positive, and would bring about an enrichment in any kind of religious practice, so long as they remained in contact with other criteria.

The third aspect is the one which might turn out to be more negative: the quest for 'profitable relationships'—that is to say, for the satisfaction of the desire that religion should be useful. Here we are bordering on the magic, superstition and fanaticism, which are a constant threat to and a frequent defect in popular piety.

Meslin's paper was criticised in the Quebec Colloquy for being based on a questionable presupposition. It presents popular religion as a reactive phenomenon, as though it only arose *a posteriori*, by way of reaction to the corruption of something which existed previously. There are writers who think that the very opposite is the case. The popular form would come first, and the secondary, later, derived form, in so far as it was opposed to the popular form, would be the official, institutional one. In this respect popular piety can be compared to popular speech, popular medicine, popular wisdom, popular music, etc. These can all be seen as primary forms from which are derived the literary language, scientific medicine, academic philosophy, etc.

It is certainly difficult to show, from the historical or chronological point of view, which is primary. What we can say is that there is a *certain dialectical relationship between the popular and non-popular* (whether it be called official, institutional, or whatever). And, above all, it is possible to make a distinction (as Van Gennep, for example, does in his various investigations into folk-lore) between what is truly popular and what is popularised— between what is originally and genuinely born from the people and what is introduced into it in different ways. Clearly what is popularised is not always negative. On the contrary, any human group which was wholly inbred culturally, and which did not have the benefit of receiving and assimilating external values, would be condemned to sterility or entropy. This would be ethnocentrism of the worst kind.

If we now set these observations in the context of a fuller and more complex description, we can indicate *nine main features* which are characteristic of popular religion.

I would place first 'the magical element', understood positively as the sense of the super-rational, the *intuitive*, the substitution of an Aristotelian or Cartesian logic of distinction and separation by a logic of participation, communication and association.

Two other typical features are 'the *symbolical*' and 'the *imaginative*'—that is to say, the sense of the image, of the association of images, the creative fantasy, etc.

A fourth feature is what we might call 'the *mystical*', understood as the powerful, emotive, living, experiential context of all the religious activities of the people, as well as the 'stretching of awareness' which is sought in them or through them.

Two further dimensions to be distinguished are 'the *festive*' and 'the *theatrical*'. Popular piety is eminently celebratory and loves the expressiveness of the total spectacle, of the multi-coloured performance, of the production which takes the street, the market-place, a section of the town, or the whole town, as its setting.

A fundamental ingredient within the festival and the spectacle is the element of farce, mockery, humour, criticism.

'The *communal*' is an eighth aspect of the piety which we are analysing. More appropriately we might describe it as its context, its essential setting. The people are grouped together in confraternities, brotherhoods, associations, to channel their religious practice. And their celebrations or festivals consist often of a general exchange of group contests, services, invitations— that is to say, of a great 'potlatch', to use the term by which such things are described in the phenomenology of religion.

The last dimension we have to mention is the *political* one. Popular religion has often contributed to the preservation of a people's self-awareness and has sometimes led to a struggle for dignity, emancipation and liberty.[9]

If we wish to analyse the phenomenon of popular religion *at greater depth*, and, at the same time, in a more concrete way, taking account of its place in the life of the Church, we shall have to distinguish *three main levels*: the first is the *anthropological* one, that profound level of a man's existence as part of the natural order and of social and family life. Here we may observe that, for example, the great religious festivals of the people are centred on the solstices (Nativity, and St. John the Baptist) and the equinoxes (Easter, the Virgin, Patrons), on the stellar phases of the agricultural work-cycle, as well as the important occasions in family life (being born, growing up, getting married, falling ill, dying).

This level clearly leads on to another deeper one—the *religious* level. The reason is simple: these cosmic, natural and human realities appear as great symbols of the transcendent, which they express and reveal. Through their power, through their life-giving and regenerative fecundity, all these realities of sun, moon, earth, fire, water, air, stone, mountain, human body (both masculine and feminine) become great hierophanies which point to the sacred and awaken the sense of mystery.

Lastly, the third level is that of the *grafting of the Christian element* on to the other two levels. The festival of 'the undefeated sun' at the winter solstice leads into the Nativity; the spring festival of the vernal equinox is converted into Easter. The rites of initiation are transformed into our sacraments of baptism, confirmation, Eucharist. And so on.[10]

This is not an opportunist, proselytising operation of appropriation by the first Christians. It is the step from creation to 'salvation history'. It is the synthesis between nature and revelation, between the cosmic and the historical, in the universal design of the one God who 'speaks to us in different ways, and, in the end, has spoken to us through his Son' (Hebrews 1:2). Life is not only a matter of fertility. It is a matter of the Easter transition from bondage to liberty, and, above all, from death to resurrection in Christ.

If this *synthesis*, which today we call encultured evangelism, is well carried out, we need speak no longer of popular religion but of *popular Catholicism*. Popular Catholicism then turns out to be a well-balanced, harmonious form of human existence, a form which today we, who belong to the so-called developed societies, long for, because we lack either the cosmic, natural dimension, or the historical-prophetic dimension.

In face of the destabilising forces in our world today, we need to recognise that at certain times and in certain places popular Catholicism has been an example of fruit in season, because it has given the people a harmonious form of existence which has been deep, experiential, satisfying, enjoyable, embracing life's most intimate realities, material and sexual, and without any repressive Manichaeism or dualism. At the same time life has been structured, committed, liberating and critical.[11]

Nevertheless in many other cases popular Catholicism is something very different, and seems to contain powerful contradictory cross-currents and a mixture of opposing values.

In *conclusion* I offer a brief summary of the *different sociological forms* in which popular Catholicism can be said to manifest itself today.

1. There are the remains of *pre-Christian*, archaic, village religions, surviving in forms which are more or less magical, superstitious, pagan or mechanical. These may be the relics of a protest against the imposition of Christianity by force, through the exercise of political power.

In Gramsci's view, these are a form of reaction on the part of oppressed, marginalised, exploited or underdeveloped classes against the dominant classes, allied, at various times, with the ecclesiastical hierarchy. This is the dialectic between dominant and subordinate religions or cultures.[12]

2. There are also a number of *popular religious forms or practices which have remained alive* and retained their strength and effectiveness from very ancient times. These are not mere relics or fossils coming to us from the past.[13]

But there exists in addition a resurgence and renascence of certain ancient rural traditions which are gaining a new lease of life (pilgrimages, patronal festivals, the Marian cult). This movement represents an effort to overcome the contradictions inherent in an industrial civilisation (uprooting, emigration, depersonalisation, being lost in the mass, anonymity).

3. In a sense we might also include in the previous category the numerous *charismatic-pentecostal groups* which are to be found everywhere, in both rural and urban settings. Their members are often peasants or urban workers, but they also include middle-class people. Here we find a longing to participate directly in a more spontaneous, more emotional or experiential way of life and form of religion, in the face of the mechanisation and standardisation of our technological society. This is what Max Weber calls the charismatic phase in religion, over against the bureaucratic institutional phase.

4. There are many groups and quasi-religious associations which form themselves into movements in search of *healing, health*. They are based on ecclesiastical models, and their leader, the healer, is like the saint. He has trances, visions, and performs healing miracles.

The explanation is similar to that for the previous section. Those who are marginalised in society, and for whom medicine is depersonalised, are seeking substitutes and reassurances.

5. A fifth category consists of *Afro-Catholic and Amerindian cults* in the American continent. Such groups are seeking to express a cultural identity repressed by colonial society and present-day capitalist-technological society.[14]

6. A form which ought to be recorded as falling within the scope of this article, in spite of its peculiarities, is that of the *popular basic communities*. In fact these communities correspond to a tradition of popular movements which were already to be found in the Church back in the fourteenth century. They were formed around groups of penitents, converts, etc. Then and now such communities have come into being as forms of denunciation of, or protest against, the Church's close links with the powerful. They represent a critical awareness of the official Church as the Church of the rich, standing over against the Church of the poor.[15]

We end our synthesis with one last classification.

The relationship between the ecclesiastical hierarchy and the people may be expressed as follows:

Ecclesiastical authority has at different times taken up four different attitudes: proposition, prescription, tolerance and proscription.

The people's reactions have been similarly varied, passing from voluntary acceptance, forced submission and syncretism, to rejection and repudiation.

Translated by G.W.S. Knowles

Notes

1. The General Secretariat of CELAM (ed.) *Medellín* (Madrid 1977). See especially Document VI on popular pastoral care.
2. J. Sobrino *Resurrección de la verdadera Iglesia. Los probres lugar teológico de la eclesiología* (Santander 1981) pp. 64–65 & 276.
3. M. Marzal *El sincretismo iberoamericano* (Lima 1985); L. Maldonado *Introducción a la Religiosidad popular* (Santander 1985); L. Maldonado *Génesis del Catolicismo popular* (Madrid 1979).
4. J.C. Scannone 'Enfoques teológico-pastorales latinoamericanos de la religiosidad popular' in *Stromata 41* (1985) 261–274.
5. *Documentos de Puebla* (Madrid 1971) pp. 131–137.
6. M. Imbert 'Les Cultures populaires: sous-produits culturels ou cultures marginalisées?' in *Les Cultures populaires* ed. G. Poujo & R. Labourié (Paris 1979) pp. 13–21.
7. V. Lanternari 'La Religion populaire. Perspective historique et anthropologique' in *Archives de sciences sociales des religions* (1982) pp. 121–143, 133.
8. M. Meslin 'Le Phénomène religieux populaire' in B. Lacroix & P. Boglioni *Les Religions populaires* (Quebec 1972).
9. A development of this phenomenology can be found in L. Maldonado *Religiosidad popular. Nostalgia de lo mágico* (Madrid 1976).
10. R. Pannet *Le Catholicisme populaire* (Paris 1974).
11. M. Eliade *Fragments d'un Journal* (Paris 1973) pp. 425, 499.

12. A. Gramsci *Letteratura e vita nazionale* (Turin 1950) p. 215; see also A. Gramsci *Quaderni del carcere*.

13. F. Cardini *I Giorni del sacro* (Novara 1983).

14. V. Lanternari 'La religion populaire' in *Archives de sciences sociales des religions 53* (1982) 121–143.

15. J.J. Tamayo *Comunidades cristianas populares* (Salamanca 1981).

Jean Delumeau

Official and Popular Religion in France during the Reformation and Counter-Reformation

THE MANY discussions of the last few years on the subject of 'popular religion' have thrown a great deal of light on the *history of Christianisation*.[1] Above all, they have led to a much more balanced understanding of the religious behaviour of the masses in past and present. For the general tendency in the past was, as Vauchez says, 'to measure religion in the middle ages by the yardstick of post-Tridentine Catholicism'.[2] Similarly, Julia states: 'The modern and contemporary reduction of the Church to the social body of its priests [had] added a new function of language to the religious field: on the one hand the articulated teaching [referred] less and less to a spiritual experience or to the life of the faithful, and instead became the ideology peculiar to the clerical group; on the other hand, an increasingly bureaucratic form of administration [controlled] cultic practices by a systematic elimination of "superstitions" and a widespread disciplinary framework'.[3]

Unconsciously, historians have allowed themselves to become prey to a clerical ideology. This is also stated by Davis: 'Historians of popular religion in Europe have acted as if their main mission was to separate the wheat from the chaff . . . . They mark out the beliefs and practices which are truly religious from those which are superstitious, and/or magical'.[4] In more recent times historians and sociologists have assisted each other in this rehabilitation of the religion of the masses. Mollat has reminded us of Lucien Febvre's statement about the Christian's day in the fifteenth-sixteenth centuries: 'To say some-

12

what scornfully that it was no more than practices is almost ridiculous'.[5]

Vauchez, to whom I shall return, asks the question which the answer conceals: 'Has Christianity lost its authenticity by popularising itself?'[6] In the same spirit Manselli stresses the 'supernatural dimension of popular religion'.[7] For the sociologists, Bonnet says that no one any longer believes that 'popular' is synonymous with 'primitive' or 'decadent' or that popular religion is more or less orthodox than élite religion.[8] Pannet makes an observation of some weight: 'No élites without a popular mass; no clergy without people'[9]—which asks us to conclude, for present and past, that the official and doctrinal form and the popular form of Christianity were and are *neither separate nor independent of one another*. Duby, moreover, draws attention to the fact that 'the Christianity of the fourteenth century received spontaneous religious attitudes from the people at a time when, under the influence of Dominican and Franciscan preachers, those in control of the Church wished to put themselves within reach of the masses. It was then that they were to take a certain number of topics and images from popular culture and to mingle them in an ideological whole which, in its forms of expression, remained entirely aristocratic'.[10] All these viewpoints tend to converge and reveal a *spirituality of the masses* which was established essentially on a basis of communitarian practices (chants, processions, pilgrimages) and informed more by liturgy—this was the case especially in the Byzantine domain—than by catechism. Whereas élites tend to conceptualise religion, their truths are rather 'received subjectively by those sectors of the population which are without access to the civilisation of script'.[11]

At any rate, we have here some elements of a casebook which for several years has *re-evaluated* what was generally considered previously, with some scorn, to be the religion of 'bumpkins' or a 'para-religion'—an expression of Philippe Ariès. The 'para-religious' are no longer the 'forgotten men and women of history'.[12]

This rehabilitation has helped to spotlight a form of *Christian magic* which was inevitable in a pre-industrial civilisation. In this respect too historians and sociologists tend to reach more or less the same opinion in many respects. Vauchez sees in 'the popular Christianisation of the thirteenth and fourteenth centuries . . . a set of practices common to religions as a whole and which are found in all traditional civilisations'.[13] Gieysztor[14] stresses the 'mixing of Christian magic and pagan magic in a single structure including both taught and lived religion and the folk background from which very old but still living beliefs arise, and deeply cohesive with the filtered contents of educated culture'. He adds that in Bohemia and Poland magical instances were not only an inheritance from pagan Slav antiquity. There were also quite new importations by the first missionary clergy; in support of this finding he cites lives of saints, *exempla* and accounts of miracles.

Throughout Catholic Europe, until a recent period, '*rituals*' offered several blessings for protecting both the marriage bed and harvests and water in the well, and exorcisms to stop storms, despatch wolves and all harmful creatures. In 1663 a vicar of the chapter of Perpignan (when the bishopric was vacant) enjoined priests under pain of prosecution not to leave their parishes during storms so that they could always be available to parishioners who would come to ask them to ring the bells against thunder and lightning and to address the threatening skies.[15] Similarly, in sixteenth-century Bohemia as in seventeenth-century Germany, the anthologies of Protestant canticles retained, clearly at the urging of the ordinary people, hymns and chants against bad weather and other natural disasters.[16] These facts have to do with the mental structures of the pre-industrial period. It was very difficult and often impossible in past centuries not to try to affect natural phenomena by means of formulas which seem to us to have nothing to do with the laws of nature. Hence this statement of Joutard in regard to the Cévennes, after a recent investigation: 'Magical beliefs seem just as varied in Protestant as in Catholic countries, ranging from fantastic beings of a more or less diabolical colour right up to such phenomena as the "evil eye" and "spells"'.[17] Why then, asks the sociologist Luneau, are revealed religions and rural traditions irreconcilable?

This revelation of the *progressive embodiment of Christianity in structures shaped a long time before its arrival* asks for some refinement of the chronology of Christianisation. Manselli wrote in this regard: 'The history of Christian life in the West [has not been] a triumphal progress but a slow and difficult advance in the consciousness of the faithful'.[18] It is no longer possible now to identify, as far as the middle ages are concerned, a *proclaimed Christianity* and an *effective Christianisation*. Medievalists stress the turning-point represented by the beginning of the thirteenth century and the founding of the mendicant Orders (and therefore the rise of preaching), and at the same time the stricter organisation of religious life which the fourth Lateran Council (1215) tried to enforce. De la Roncière in respect of the Florentine *contado* of before 1348,[19] Gieysztor for southern Poland of the fourteenth-fifteenth centuries,[20] Rapp in regard to Germany in the same period,[21] and, together with them, Duby[22] and Mollat[23] on a more general level, stress the fact that Christianity became henceforth a *popular religion* and one lived not only by sparse élites, which would seem to have been the case beforehand.

Do the above arguments and deductions really go to show that, at least at the end of the middle ages, *Christianity and Christianisation had become virtually the same thing*?

Or must we on the contrary support Schmitt in his emphasis on the conflict of cultures and the operation of each of them, and in his conclusion that the 'Church at the very most partially Christianised a folk culture which only disappeared with the entire mode of production of which it was a part'?[24]

In *Montaillou* Le Roy Ladurie[25] states that the peasants of Sabarthès knew the *Our Father* at least by hearsay, were aware of transsubstantiation and the existence of the Virgin Mary, and to a certain extent observed the fast-days imposed by the Church. It would seem above all that their Christianity was, 'loosely' indeed, but definitely, centred on the concept of salvation and the 'absolution of the dying and the redemption of sin'; on the notion that the 'souls of the dying who have repented of their sins are as bright as light'. Hence the 'saving virtue of confession and contrition before death: this was the fundamental common denominator at that time of all religious belief in the Comté de Foix'. After making these points, Le Roy Ladurie does not seek to hide the complex nature of the actual religious situation. 'But frequent as all these references were, for the people of Montaillou the crucifix remained virtually unoccupied. In Sabarthès only a minority of sealots . . . went in for macabre meditation upon Christ's suffering on the cross.' Mass was experienced as a 'mechanical practice'. Jesus in his passion was neither the object of a fervent cult nor of a Christic identification. Le Roy Ladurie also speaks of the 'popular prestige' of baptism, and says that the folklore of the Comté de Foix was scarcely Christian and had a strong tendency to paganism; many of the Occitan people held to a kind of *pagano-biblical syncretism*. There was also widespread unbelief among 'male bumpkins' elsewhere.

Ultimately, the Sabarthès we come to know is less Christianised than seemed the case initially. That is not to offer a value-judgement but to seek to characterise the factual situation. It also means making a functional semantic distinction: even in a Christian region 'religious' and 'Christian' were not and are not necessarily synonymous terms. That is as true of the Cathars of centuries past as of certain present-day Mexican and Afro-Brazilian cults.

We are compelled to extend our inquiry *into the limits of Christianisation in every age* and especially in that preceding the rise of the Protestant Reformation. Recent research has shown incontestably, as I stated in the foregoing, that between 1200 and 1500 Christianity had passed beyond the realm of clerical aristocracy to become the lived faith of an increasing number of lay-people, to such an extent that several of them, such as Calvin, did not scruple to undertake governance of the religious life of their contemporaries. There is no longer any doubt that Christianisation increasingly overflowed from the towns to the countryside, and that painted and sculpted images tended more and more to assist the spread of a teaching which stressed sin, death, the Judgment, the passion of Christ, the intercession of the Virgin Mary, indulgences, and so forth.

Do we nevertheless have enough information to confirm the large-scale *Christianisation of the countryside* at this time: that is, a minimal awareness of the doctrine and ethics of Christianity? Surely our documentation necessarily refers essentially to the towns? Most often, we are forced to ask ourselves what we really know for certain about the religious life of the rural world in which the vast majority of the population lived.

We know that the *evangelisation by the mendicant Orders* was decisive in the urban environment. But it was certainly much more sporadic in the countryside. Martin says in respect of the Brittany of the thirteenth to fifteenth centuries: 'We have very little information by which to assess the penetration of the rural environment by religious Orders. Most countryfolk encountered mendicant friars, preachers and indulgence sellers very infrequently'.[26] Surely this was the case elsewhere.

On the other hand, are we merely to discard the numerous texts—both Catholic and Protestant—of the sixteenth and seventeenth centuries which describe *various areas of Europe as 'Indies' of the interior*? The expression—which became a multi-denominational stereotype—seems as appropriate to southern Italy[27] as to the Dauphiné[28] and the British Isles (Wales, Lancashire, Yorkshire, Scotland, Devon,[29] and so on)—a quite incomplete list. Some people will object that this is tantamount to reverting to the religion of the clergy who judged their contemporaries strictly from the heights of their knowledge and their own religious example. And that is indeed the case. But then why should we, in our turn, by means of an equivalent psychological gesture on the basis of our own knowledge, reject *in toto* the witness of Catholic and Protestant churchmen alike merely because they happened to belong to the dominant culture? Michel Vovelle is justified in writing: 'Reformers of all persuasions in the sixteenth century had more than a phantom to contend with' (=a scarcely Christianised popular culture).[30]

On the other hand, when we read so many documents regarding the 'religious ignorance' of times past, we may forget that Christianity is grounded on a *Book*, and that this Book proffers simultaneously *a Revelation and a model, who is Jesus*. To be sure, this Revelation and this model may be excellently received and assimilated by virtue of oral transmission and an iconographical and liturgical form of instruction which was accessible to Villon's illiterate mother. But I think I can detect behind the constant complaints of the churchmen the fact that in a certain number of areas, especially rural sectors, the Christian memory functioned poorly and brought about major obliterations both of the message and of the model. The result was a fierce campaign against what the rulers of the Church deemed to be 'paganism' and 'superstition'.

A study of the *limits of Christianisation in the past* also forces the historian to examine the *marginal types of former times*. In fact research is now very much taken up with them, for, from the thirteenth century onwards there was a surge in Western society of the number of the 'unstable, impoverished and undesirable',[31] and of all kinds of vagabonds and displaced persons who constantly wandered from the country towards the towns and *vice versa*, right up to the industrial revolution.[32] An attempt to assess the extent of this serious social phenomenon necessarily also involves measurement of the real dimensions of a scarcely Christianised universe.

There are yet *other avenues to be explored* by anyone wishing to investigate the limits of Christianisation in the past. Lucien Febvre's book on *Unbelief in the Sixteenth Century* no longer seems so convincing as it did thirty-eight years ago. He certainly underestimated the rejections of and indifference to Christianity in past societies. Le Roy Ladurie, in *Montaillou*, questions Febvre's thesis on the non-existence of atheism before the seventeenth century; at Sabarthès he discovered an artisan, a woman and a peasant who declared that the world had neither beginning nor end, that 'there was no other age than our own', and that the 'soul was only blood'.[33] Here we have a rural naturalism which runs counter to received opinion. Ginzburg's incisive study, *Il Formaggio e i vermi* (the world of a sixteenth-century miller), tends in the same direction. Menocchio, says Ginzburg, 'went to confession (outside his village, admittedly), went to communion, and had certainly had his children baptized. Nevertheless, he did not accept a divine Creation, the Incarnation, or Redemption. He denied the saving efficacy of the sacraments. He said that to love one's neighbour was more important than love of God. He believed that the whole world was God'.[34]

I think that, after due research, historiographers will discover other testimonies of this kind and that, in any case, we should think hard about the *fear of blasphemy* evinced by the church culture at the beginning of the modern era. This subject is in fact under examination.[35] In the sixteenth century and afterwards, the authorities of Western and central Europe as a whole were extraordinarily singleminded in their conviction that their contemporaries were given to swearing and blaspheming on a vast and unprecedented scale.[36]

Finally, in two other research fields which are close to the foregoing, surely we cannot ignore the *status of hypocrisy*—always with a religious connotation—in the literature of Christianity, and surely we should not unthinkingly accept the various testimonies which go to make up a conformist image; that is, a religious practice obedient to established norms and more suffered than desired and vital. In his *Apology of Raimond Sebon* Montaigne wrote:

'... we receive our religion only in our own way and by our own hands and in no other manner than other religions are received. We came into contact with it in the country where it was the general practice ... We are Christians in the same way in which we are inhabitants of the Périgord or Germans.'

I recommend, therefore, the general idea of a *gradual Christianisation* which was relatively slow to take on and quite varied in its effects. I would refine this statement by way of the following three propositions: 1. In Europe at the beginning of the sixteenth century everyday religion, it would seem, was permeated by a considerable amount of Christian or Christianised magism which was capable of reconciliation with a wholly 'authentic' Christian life (the criteria for which nevertheless require careful definition); 2. There would not seem to be any evidence of structured forms of resistance to Christianity in the form of diabolical sects; 3. This absence of forms of collective opposition does not signify any non-existence of individual instances of contestation, which were sometimes fleeting and often more experienced than conceptualised; nor that the Christian message was assimilated by all populations. Indeed, the extent of non-Christianisation varied according to time, locality and social level, but was always there.

Translated by J.G. Cumming

Notes

1. See especially, in addition to the works cited in the following notes, *Società, chiesa e vita religiosa nell'Ancien Régime* ed. C. Russo (Naples 1976); B. Plongern and R. Pannet *Le Christianisme populaire. Les dossiers de l'histoire* (Paris 1976); *La Religion populaire. Approches historiques* ed. B. Plongeron (Paris 1976); H. Mottu 'Critique théologique de la religion et religion populaire' *Bull. du Centre d'études protestantes* (Feb. 1977); *La Religion populaire*, international colloquium (Paris October 1977, 1979); J. Simard 'Un Patrimoine méprise. La religion populaire des Québéquois' *Cahiers du Québec* (1979).

2. A. Vauchez, conclusion of *Cahier de Fanjeaux* no. 11, *La Religion populaire en Languedoc (XIIe-XIV siècles* (Toulouse 1976) p. 434.

3. D. Julia 'A propos des sources écrites e a religion populaire: questions de méthode *Ricerche di Storia sociale e religiosa* 11 (Jan.–June 1977) p. 111.

4. N.Z. Davis 'Some tasks and themes in the study of popular religion' in C. Trinkhaus *The Pursuit of Holiness* (Leyden 1974) p. 307.

5. M. Mollat 'Les Formes populaires de la piété au Moyen Age' *Actes du 99e Congrès national des sociétés savantes* (Besancon 1974; Paris 1977) p. 23.

6. A. Vauchez 'Eglise et vie religieuse au Moyen Age' *Annales ESC* (July-August 1973).

7. R. Manselli *La Religion populaire au Moyen Age* (Montreal & Paris 1975) p. 87.

8. Fr Bonnet's intervention during the colloquium at the ATP Museum (October 1977) *La Religion populaire* (Paris 1974) p. 15.

10. G. Duby 'Histoire sociale et histoire des mentalités. Univers mental du passe' *Nouvelle Critique* (May 1970).

11. J. Paul 'La Religion populaire au Moyen Age' *RHEF* 63 No 170 (Jan.-June 1977) p. 83.

12. P. Ariès 'Religion populaire et reformes religieuses' *La Maison-Dieu* 122 (1975) p. 96.

13. A. Vauchez, conclusion to *Cahier de Fanjeaux* No. 11, p. 439.

14. 'Les mentalités religieuses populaires en Pologne et en Bohême médiévales' *L'Histoire vécue du peuple chrétien* ed. J. Delumeau (Toulouse 1979) pp. 315-329.

15. J. Delumeau *La Peur en Occident (XIVe-XVIIIe siècles)* (Paris nd) p. 66.

16. Articles by M.E. Ducreux and B. Vogler in *L'Histoire vécue du peuple chrétien*, cited in note 14.

17. P. Joutard 'Protestantisme populaire et univers magique: le cas cénévol' *Le Monde alpin et rhodanien* (1977) p. 145.

18. R. Manselli *La Religion populaire* the work cited in note 7, at p. 188.

19. *Histoire vécue du peuple chrétien* I pp. 381 and 417.

20. *Ibid.* I pp. 315-329.

21. *Ibid.* I pp. 335-355.

22. G. Duby *Fondements d'un nouvel humanisme, 1220-1440* (Geneva 1966) p. 88.

23. M. Mollat 'Les Formes populaires . . . ' the article cited in note 5 above, at p. 21.

24. J.-C. Schmitt 'Religion populaire et culture folklorique' *Annales ESC* (Sept.-Oct. 1976) p. 948.

25. For all the following see E. Le Roy Ladurie *Montaillou: village occitan de 1294 a 1324* (Paris 1975): ET: *Montaillou: Cathars and Catholics in a French Village 1294-1324* (London 1978) esp. ch. XVIII and XIX.

26. H. Martin *Les Ordres mendiants en Bretagne (vers 1230-1530)* (Paris 1975) p. 402.

27. *Storia d'Italia*, I: *I caratteri originali* (Turin 1972) pp. 656-658.

28. Here I draw on the work in progress of B. Dompnier for his thesis on the *Missions et Prédications en Dauphiné au XVIIe siècle.*

29. C. Hill *Change and Continuity in Seventeenth Century England* (London 1974) esp. ch. I.

30. M. Vovelle 'La Religion populaire: problèmes et methodes' in *Le Monde alphin et rhodanien* (1977) pp. 7-31.

31. J. Le Goff 'Le Dossier des mendiants' *1274: année charnière: mutations et continuité* (1974 colloquium) (Paris 1978).

32. Bibliographical references on this point are to be found in M. Mollat *Les pauvres au Moyen Age* (Paris 1978) pp. 367-389.

33. E. Le Roy Ladurie *Montaillou* the work cited in note 25, at pp. 525-535.

34. C. Ginzburg *Il formaggio e i vermi: il cosmo di un mugnaio del' 500* (Turin 1976).

35. Thesis in progress of Mme Piozza-Donati.

36. J. Delumeau *La Peur en Occident*, the work cited in note 15, above, final ch.

Wladyslaw Piwowarski

The Guarantor of National Identity: Polish Catholicism

INTRODUCTION

IN POLAND historians and sociologists have put forward the hypothesis that Polish Catholicism as a mass expression of religious feeling has for many centuries guaranteed national identity. There is nevertheless a lack of detailed studies, particularly in the historical field, that could verify this hypothesis exactly. Catholic historiography in Poland is more concerned with describing the structures and functions of ecclesiastical institutions than with analysing the connections between the various religious and social phenomena. Hence it is only to a limited extent that conclusions about the causes and mechanisms of the influence of Catholicism can be applied to Polish society.

Studies carried out at the time when Poland was celebrating the thousandth anniversary of its conversion were most frequently concerned with the significance and role of Marian veneration in the history of the Polish nation.[1] The result of these studies has been to provide a wealth of material not only covering the influence of Polish Catholicism on the national identity but also describing the characteristics of this Catholicism.

This essay will in part draw on the results of these historical researches, although confining itself to sociological analysis. From the sociological point of view what is of interest is the hypothesis that Polish Catholicism, both in the past and in the present, functions on two levels: the national level and the level of daily life. On the first level it is the 'faith of the nation' and on the second the 'religion of life'.[2] Although these two concepts of J. Majka are to be understood in a different sense from that used here, they nevertheless seem extremely useful for the hypothesis that has been put forward.

The faith of the nation has not changed in Poland. Practically everyone is a believer: the proportion of those who practise their religion is now over 90 per cent. At this level Polish Catholicism guarantees national identity. As the faith of the nation it is secularised and indicates what is involved with the particular situation the nation finds itself in. This faith counts 'as that which holds society together, its principle of integration. Or as that which gives it its identity, what for a large group of people who feel that they belong together symbolises the meaning of their common life or what for the individual makes the unavoidable suffering of his or her life tolerable'.[3]

With the religion of life it is a different matter. It is the religion that is experienced and realised in daily life (*religion vécue*). At this level it is subject to transformations, and these in different directions—similar to developments that can be observed in developed societies. An example of this is the selective religious feeling that in Poland comprises the chief tendency of such transformations.

In this essay we shall concentrate exclusively on the first level, in other words on the faith of the nation, since this provides the point of reference for the analyses. To begin with we shall deal with the characteristics and role of Catholicism in the history of Poland and then we shall tackle the analysis of the situation of Polish Catholicism with reference to values and religious rites at the national level.

1. THE CHARACTERISTICS AND ROLE OF CATHOLICISM IN THE HISTORY OF POLAND

It is instructive to investigate how and when the present model of Polish Catholicism took shape and what role it fulfilled in history.

Historians have shown that the present model of Polish Catholicism has undergone a profound evolution. It did not acquire settled features before the sixteenth and seventeenth centuries, in other words at the time of the Reformation and Counter-Reformation.[4] From the start this model was spread among the landed gentry, who looked for their own identity in it (*ideologia sarmacka*). Under the influence of the landed gentry it was also adopted by the broad mass of the peasantry and by the entire nation.

The characteristics of the model of Polish Catholicism have been described in various ways by historians and analysts of culture.[5] The most important of them are the following:

(a) The close *connection between religion and patriotism* in which the second value is placed higher than the first. Religion was turned into a means and served as such in the struggle for patriotic goals, for example during national uprisings.

(b) The *emotional link* with the 'faith of our fathers' without an intellectual foundation. Predominant were fideism and also social commitment in the various forms of religious life. Immediate experiences of the moment and bold decisions took precedence over the systematic and persevering realisation of the ideals of the Gospel. Thus, for example, people liked to take part in pilgrimages and retreats, when they made emotional decisions which however they often did not put into effect in daily life.

(c) *Marian spirituality.* On the one hand Mary was regarded as the queen and protectress of the people, while on the other the people surrendered to her completely, to the point of becoming her 'slaves'.

(d) *Ritualism*, expressed in mass rites. The Catholic Church in Poland has on several occasions held coronations of icons of Our Lady. In 1717 the icon of Our Lady of Częstochowa was crowned. From this date the title of patron and queen of Poland was applied to the Black Madonna of Częstochowa. After this event other icons of Our Lady in various other places were crowned. These coronations were often mass demonstrations. There were also other opportunities for large assemblies of people and demonstrations, as for example Church and national feast-days and pilgrimages. Religious practice was always more important than religious doctrine. From time immemorial Poles have identified themselves more by their behaviour than by dogmas with their religion.

(e) *Service to the nation.* In Poland Catholicism has always fulfilled a wide range of functions. This means that it has had influence not only with regard to the message of religion but also in various fields of secular life, for example the economy, education and leisure. Because of the broad scope of the Church's activities the clergy have enjoyed higher prestige and confidence among the people.

The characteristics of Polish Catholicism that have been mentioned form the foundation of national identity. Catholicism integrated all social classes, served the entire nation and always remained within society.

This model of Polish Catholicism also found its expression in the individual role it exercised particularly during periods when, thanks to partition and occupation, the nation was without a State. During these periods religious and national values became even more closely linked with each other than before. This meant that betrayal of the nation was experienced as betrayal of religion and *vice versa.*[6]

Polish Catholicism always fulfilled a *critical function* with regard to the political powers-that-be. This led to some bishops and many priests being persecuted. They made similar sacrifices to the whole nation. It is interesting that in the last few centuries there have always been fresh martyrs who have been honoured by the entire nation. They were regarded as national victims but also as symbols of the nation's unity and future freedom. This applies in particular to the heroes of the national uprisings and wars.

Polish Catholicism also always fulfilled a *caring function* with regard to the nation. This found expression in its nurturing of the Polish language, of Polish customs, traditions, culture, etc. When the nation was forced to keep silent it was the Church that articulated its needs and problems.

In particular Polish Catholicism fulfilled an *integrative function*. It involved people everywhere where there was the opportunity to demonstrate their religion and patriotism publicly, for example the anniversaries of the various uprisings, of the constitution of 3 May, of national feasts. All these opportunities have brought the people together and have effectively demonstrated that they all belong to one nation.

It is characteristic that the same model of Catholicism exists in Poland after the second world war and that, despite changes both planned and spontaneous, it fulfils the same role in the nation. Just as in the past it is the maker and guarantor of national identity, and this beyond its own values and religious rites.

2. VALUES AND NATIONAL IDENTITY

In Poland's situation it is necessary to distinguish between those values that serve *man's ultimate orientation* and those that *give society or the State their basic orientation*. As a socialist State Poland is not ideologically neutral. This means that since the second world war this State needed and looked for an ideological unity. In keeping with Marxist ideology everyone in Poland was meant to be an atheist because only this ideology was regarded as scientifically based. The socialist State is thus not an 'elective society' but a 'fated society':[7] people have no alternatives, no possibilities of choice, no pluralism. Their destiny is fixed, not just with regard to their economic, social and political life but also with regard to their philosophy of life and thus in the field where because of his dignity man transcends all earthly institutions.

From the start this *ideology was suspect in Poland*—not just for religious but also for cultural reasons. In Poland Catholicism forms part of the national culture. Even if it is not unconditionally an individual value it is certainly a general value (the common good). In this way socialism as an atheist system did not fit into the national culture. In comparison with Polish national culture it counted as something imported from outside.

In this situation it is not the socialist State but *Catholicism that can guarantee national identity*. After the second world war various circles in Polish society still believed in socialism. They thought this social and political system would bring about social justice and equality. In the course of time these people became more and more disillusioned and came to realise that ideology and reality never coincided. When people observed and experienced this they committed themselves ever more strongly to Catholicism, which represented their only chance. That is why the proportion of believers and of practising Catholics is so high in Poland.

Beyond the values touching the meaning of life we need to consider also the basic values of society. These values are very important for every State that wants to exist. Without agreement on these values a State has no future.

In the past in Poland two of these values were particularly emphasised, religion and patriotism. Since the second world war the area of these values has broadened. In times of unrest—and thus in 1956, 1968, 1970, 1974, 1980—people have fought not only for bread but also for such social and ethical values as the dignity of the individual, human rights, justice, truth, and solidarity.

This was confirmed by a survey carried out by a Catholic weekly this year.[8] Those taking part in this survey (182 people in all) were answering the question why they had come back. They said they had been converted, had come back to the faith, to God, to the Church, because they had discovered the higher values which they could accept and with which they could identify. A typical answer was: 'I have come back to the Church because in it I have found once again the values I had lost', or: 'Because in the Church I feel myself united with the nation'.

People in Poland want to reach a consensus; but this is impossible. Hence Polish society is undergoing a prolonged period of *anomie*.[9] If there is no agreement, force and a state of war rule. Polish Catholicism supports all the fundamental values of society that in recent times people have become aware of. Hence the Catholic Church guarantees the national identity. More than this, it has been able to mediate in the dialogue between the State and the nation. But this has been impossible because the conditions for an authentic dialogue do not exist. A recent example of this has been the Solidarity movement.

3. RELIGIOUS RITES AND NATIONAL IDENTITY

For years *religious rites have played a major role* in the Polish nation, but nevertheless this role has become much greater after the seond world war. In a country where religious organisations are forbidden a variety of religious practices have developed—and done so at national, regional and local levels. The motivation for taking part in religious mass demonstrations is not just religious but also political and patriotic. They have not come together so much because they are devout believers but rather because they are against the règime and want to show their patriotism.

Among the best known mass events in Poland are the coronations of icons of Our Lady that have already been mentioned, the visiting of dioceses and parishes by the icon of the Black Madonna of Częstochowa, the pilgrimages, jubilee celebrations during the nine years of preparation for the thousandth anniversary of the coming of Christianity to Poland, Corpus Christi processions, the two visits by Pope John Paul II, and the Masses for the Fatherland after the suppression of Solidarity. All these major events are linked with religious and national symbols.

With these should be counted other phenomena that play a role at the national level, in other words the presence of religious symbols in public life, as for example the struggle over having crosses in schools, the great readiness of people to make sacrifices for Church purposes (over 85 per cent of the population), and the building of churches throughout the country. The Minister for Religious Affairs, Adam Lopatka, had this to say about Lublin: 'Since what is termed Poland's baptism, or more precisely since Lublin was founded in the fourteenth century, up to the nineteenth century twelve churches were built in this city. In the nineteenth century no churches were built, and in the twentieth century, in the period between the two world wars, only three churches were built in this city, and those of wood. In contrast to this permission has now been granted for building more than ten (seventeen) sacred edifices, and thus for more than have been built during the last thousand years.[10] This statement also illustrates the situation in Poland of recent years when there have been great difficulties over building churches. There is only one diocese—Przemyśl—which has built more than 200 new churches in the 1960s and 1970s without State permission.

An important role in the field of religious rites was played by the *late Cardinal Stefan Wyszyński*. He initiated many mass events, particularly those connected with the cult of the Black Madonna. On the basis of these he wanted on the one hand to neutralise the negative influences of the process of secularisation, on the other to unite and integrate the nation. Even the

Marxists acknowledge that he achieved both goals.

His successor, Cardinal Józef Glemp, continues this role. It is impossible to be the head of the Church in Poland without supporting the faith of the nation. Hence he uses every opportunity to take part in mass events and also tries to unite Poles and integrate them. But it is not easy, because the political and national goals are always valued more highly than the religious and ecclesiastical ones.

By means of all the events that have been mentioned Polish Catholicism has deepened national consciousness and identified the people with the nation. Religious practices are in reality demonstrations on behalf of the nation. By means of these rites nearly all Poles bear witness that they are united and integrated and beyond this that they have found the meaning of their life together and have made their unavoidable sufferings tolerable.

CONCLUSION

Because of historical conditions and the present political situation Polish Catholicism is the guarantor of national identity. Historically there developed a unique model of this Catholicism which also played a unique role in the nation. For years Poles did not have a State of their own but were persecuted by foreign political powers. Hence they identified themselves with Catholicism.

Since the end of the second world war the situation has been much the same, and this has had its effects particularly with regard to values and behaviour as well as with regard to human relationships. This situation has led to *anomie* and protests. The changes that nationally were looked for in the direction of freedom, autonomy and justice did not come about. Poles remained disillusioned, frustrated and bereft of hope. Because of this they seek further support in Catholicism, which is the guarantor not just of national identity but also of human dignity and human rights. These two tendencies have become closely interlinked especially in the last few years.

But in this case Polish Catholicism functions much more in public than in private life. This means that it is experienced above all as a common good. To put it another way, for the majority of Poles it operates on the national level. Hence one can describe it as secularised and public.

Translated from the author's German by Robert Nowell

Notes

1. See J.J. Kopec 'Uwarunkowania historyczno-kulturowe czci Bogarodzicy w polskiej religijnosci' in *Religijnosc ludowa—ciaglosc i zmiana* ed. W. Piwowarski (Wroclaw 1983) pp. 21–25.

2. J. Majka 'Historyczno-kulturowe uwarunkowania katolicyzmu polskiego' in *Chrzescijanin w swiecie* 12 No. 10 (1980) 39.

3. F.X. Kaufmann 'Der Ort Gottes in unserer Kultur. Die Differenz von Religions- und Gottes-frage in der Gegenwart' in *Herder-Korrespondenz* 39 (1985) 330.

4. J.J. Kopec, the article cited in note 1, at p. 62.

5. See Z.T. Wierzbicki 'Tradycyjna religijnosc wiejska. Studium porownawcze' in *Roczniki Nauk Spolecznych* 7 (1979) 115–176.

6. J. Majka, the article cited in note 1, at pp. 39–40, and his 'Kosciol jako opozycja moralna' in *Chrzescijanin w swiecie* 14 No. 7 (1982) 3.

7. See P.L. Berger *Der Zwang zur Häresie. Religion in der pluralistischen Gesellschaft* (Frankfurt-am-Main 1980) pp. 38–39.

8. See J. Rakowiecki 'Swiadectwa. Podsumowanie ankiety "Dlaczego przychodze"' in *Tygodnik Powszechny* 34 No. 34 (1985) 4.

9. This concept comes from Émile Durkheim and means a profound disruption of society in the field of culture (the disintegration of the hierarchy of values and of the ideas of value) and in the field of structure (the dis-integration of social links). *Anomie* can be overcome by a new consensus and by new social ties between men and women.

10. Adam Lopatka 'Polityka wyznaniowa w PRL' in *Zagadnienia i materialy* No 4 (1983) p. 19.

Cristian Parker

Popular Religion and Protest against Oppression: The Chilean Example

1. IS RELIGION THE 'OPIUM OF THE PEOPLE'?

HOW ALIENATING is religion and popular religion in particular? This has been the central question in the discussion of many critical interpretations of religion. Indeed, the classial Marxist definition of religion as the 'opium of the people' is the ever-present background to any sociological analysis of popular religion.[1] However in an under-developed and mainly Catholic continent like Latin America, religion persists and even acquires a renewal of meaning among the masses. The function of protest against oppression performed by religion in many instances of popular struggle and resistance, forces us to reconsider the problem.

Until not long ago many Latin American intellectuals—children of an enlightened modernity—saw popular religion as a *heap of pure prejudices*, superstitions and atavisms—the 'illusory' components of an alienated consciousness—needing to be overcome by rational criticism. Recently certain theological and pastoral trends have attempted to *rediscover* the 'soul of the people' in traditional popular religion, that deeper Latin American identity opposed to liberal and Marxist secularism. Against this, there is the liberating approach which attempts to find the seeds of liberation in a religion of the oppressed challenging the dominant culture.

Taking a sociological view, we want to outline a *different interpretation of the phenomenon of religion* among the peoples of Latin America, with the *case of Chile as an example.*

28

From a sociological viewpoint religion can be seen as a form of *symbolico-cultural production characterised by its self-reference to a transcendent reality.* In this view the meanings and functions of religious people are relative to the specific times and situations of the social actors who produce and reproduce this conjunction of codified senses. Our fundamental hypothesis holds that the people, as historico-social agent, collectively produces its symbolico-religious representations and practices, by means of a process which manifests both the people's oppression and their relative autonomy. This becomes apparent in different ways according to people's relative position in the class structure and in the field of religion. By means of a process of meaning-production, which both conditions and is conditioned, the different sectors and subordinate classes express through their manifold religious activities, a *symbolic protest.* This protest is not always an open one, and only in a few cases, according to historical and structural circumstances, does it manage to constitute an authentic class consciousness in the proletarian and sub-proletarian masses. The complementary thesis holds that the alienating elements in popular religion, when such are to be found, are never of the *essence* but have their *existence* in particular social and historical circumstances.

2. RELIGION AS RESIGNATION IN THE FACE OF OPPRESSION: AN INCOMPLETE VISION

In the search for satisfaction of basic needs those who belong to the people are subordinated to their situation as a dominated class. The daily life of the working classes and the mass of under-employed and unemployed and their families in under-developed and dependent countries is marked by exploitation and deprivation. Given that capitalist society denies them their legitimate rights and deprives them of opportunities for work and welfare, the people have no alternative but to resort to a series of 'strategies for survival'.

It is precisely in this context that popular religion—often—acquires its meaning as a *parallel and complementary form of symbolic 'strategy for survival'.*

Thus in accordance with a more or less current[2] interpretation, religion is a sort of supplementary symbolic medium in the people's struggle for daily subsistence. Animism and magic are merely religio-pragmatic mechanisms with the aim of controlling and regulating surrounding events. The endemic social insecurity and chronic dependence of the poor is thus made up for by resorting to the available symbolic acts offered by belief in the miraculous powers of God, the Virgin, the saints and 'souls'. Popular religiosity takes on the character of a supernatural power to help the individual and bring him or her benefits denied by society, or else consolation in frustration.

Religion acts as a factor of adaptation to domination and reinforces the fatalism of the 'poverty culture' (D. Lewis). According to this interpretation, popular religion constitutes an important factor in popular resignation and alienation.

In certain respects this analysis is right. However, recent historical experience among Chilean popular classes and studies on religion and subordinate classes in Latin America[3] show the impossibility of applying this type of interpretation universally.

Apart from certain common characteristics, it is not possible to reduce the various heterogenous forms of religious expression in different popular groups to a *single general formula*. 'Popular Catholicism' which used to be synonymous in Latin America with a common traditional form of religiosity, also containing bits of magic, is no longer spread throughout the continent in a homogenous form. Neither does there appear to be a lack of internal integration or the incoherence of irrational thinking in the complex and multiple structure of popular symbolism.

3. DIFFERENT MODELS WHICH ARTICULATE HETEROGENOUS RELIGIOUS REPRESENTATIONS

An in-depth analysis of popular urban discourse about religion reveals this existence of *different religious models*. There is a combination of semantic categories which shape typical codes of religious meaning. The nature of these models is revealed in the language they use, grammar, vocabulary, and the whole set of popular rites and gestures. This is a religious production in a culture which does not elaborate its cultural productions in a systematic form and which engages in a constant symbolic and practical transaction with the official religion of the churches.

We do not have space here to analyse in depth the content, significance and functions of each of the models we mention. We merely note the fact that the heterogeneity of codified religious representations appears to be greater among the people in towns than in the country. As well as the persistence of more traditional models of Catholicism, we may find a model that is traditional but which differs from official Catholicism on more than one essential point (e.g. they do not believe in an after-life). There are also models originating from dissidence from Catholicism, whereas in the country Catholicism is supreme. We refer to certain models, which are formally Catholic but internally secularised and substantially sceptical and rationalist, which have doubts about a whole series of traditional official beliefs. And as well as these, there are the models which have, more or less openly, broken away from Catholicism: the popular Protestant sects and churches (e.g. popular pentecostalism), or syncretic cults such as Umbanda, Landomble, Voodoo etc, which exist especially in popular urban environments in countries strongly influenced by a population of African origin.

Among popular religious models closest to post-conciliar Catholicism, we distinguish *two principal ones*. On the one hand there is a model which has largely assimilated the pastoral renovations but whose ethical content still remains influenced by bourgeois asceticism. On the other hand there is a model with an ethic of militant commitment to justice and neighbourly love.

4. THE PLURAL FUNCTIONS OF THE RELIGIOUS IN POPULAR CULTURE

In general terms it is possible to state that the more traditional religious models fulfil certain functions at distinct levels within situations on the margin of the dominant capitalist process of production: sub-proletariat and improverished exploited masses. On the one hand—and here we see the analysis given above in operation—these religious models serve as a *symbolic protective shield* against adversity in a state of instability of employment, over-exploitation and extreme poverty. On the other hand, the fact that they reproduce traditional codes in the context of a modern society has the *internal* function of reproducing a minimum of *collective identity* in the face of invasion by the dominant culture. Thus this kind of religiosity can be considered also as a form of *passive resistance* towards the official culture and religion on the symbolic level. However—in an apparently contradictory way—religio-popular models of this kind operate in their relation to the *outside* as a prop for the established order, as factors of resignation and alienation and thus encourage a global fatalism towards domination.

Traditional religion within popular culture turns on an axis of representation in which the actor is heteronomous. God and his agents intervene providentially where required in daily life and they are the guarantee assuring the processes of reproduction and survival in poverty and oppression.

In certain segments of the subproletariat and the subproletarised lower middle class, who have slightly better access to means of subsistence, there are symbolic representations of the social order of a pre-critical type (they question domination but they do not manage to explain its causes). In interaction with these there are religious representations of a traditional type, or even of a more 'rationalist' kind. These are among working class people who generally work 'for themselves': pedlars, self-employed workers, small retail traders etc, who are nevertheless always subject formally and indirectly to capital and directly to market and economic trends. Although they are formally independent, in fact they are objectively a subordinate class.

Here religious representations—both traditional and more rationalist— have different meanings and functions. In the short term the individual seeks for subsistence, for which he counts on resorting to the meta-social and the transcendent. The religious, directly or indirectly, contributes to the symbolic resolution of real-life contradictions. But at the same time the religious models laterally reinforce a particular cultural identity, an implicit form of protest against the official culture and religion. In fact both the traditional religious model and the more rationalist one, over and above the substantial differences between them, are very far from the official Church.

Models of popular religions with a greater ethical content (which reformulate and sometimes reject popular traditions) are of *two kinds*. There is the more *individualist model* of faith which reinforces a spirit of asceticism directed towards the social promotion of the individual, which occurs in certain proletarian or sub-proletarian sectors among the better educated young. Or there is the *ethico-social model* which goes with a class consciousness in those sectors of the industrial or administrative proletariat, who through workers' organisations and trade union struggle, have acquired a critical view of capitalist society and want to change it. In the latter the ethico-utopian teaching of Christianity is articulated in a coherent form together with a consciousness of class solidarity. In its search for justice it reinterprets Christian values of salvation in function of the historical transformation of society. This type of popular religion which has 'opted for the poor' has had a strong influence in Chile and Latin America as a whole.

5. FACTOR OF PROTEST DEPENDING ON THE HISTORICAL MOMENT

This description of the heterogeneity and complexity of the daily religious productions among the people shows that the functions of symbolic protest by popular religion reaches different levels and often the historical moment only influences the form of its manifestation. If the Christian people during the Pinochet regime has demonstrated in various ways against oppression and defended life against the violation of human rights,[4] this can be seen as a form of contemporary actualisation of the potential for protest contained within popular religion.

The religion of subordinate classes, whose articulation depends on other socio-cultural representations corresponding to the situation of each class, may have various social functions. These sometimes appear exclusively, sometimes in parallel and they may even co-exist in a contradictory manner within popular culture. Factor of alienation, factor of popular identity and symbolic opposition to the official religion and culture, finally an ethical reinforcement for an attempt at social advancement or an attempt to transform society: popular religion may or may not be either of these depending on the social and historical situation.

If we look at it in the abstract using classical tools of interpretation, the people's religion can be considered in some cases as a mere reproduction of elements of official religion and the dominant culture. In this case the people would play a passive role of 'consumer' or 'user' of a religious production elaborated from beyond them and without their participation.[5] On the other hand, looked at carefully from the viewpoint of the popular classes, their *own* production of religion represents a way of recovering meaning and dignity to face a life of poverty and oppression which is otherwise a nonsense.

In the history of popular religion in the case of Chile, as in various similar cases in Latin America, the *functions of protest* are manifested differently in every historical period. The resistance of the natives to Spanish colonisation acquires the character of a symbolic drama in the course of which the natives formally accept the religion of the conquistadors, but secretly keep their belief and rites in their new syncretic cult. Towards the middle of the nineteenth century the peasantry produced a series of mythical and poetico-musical expressions (some as 'divine verses') which contain a series of covert protests against the rich.[6] The rich man accumulates wealth and humiliates the poor because he has a pact with the devil. According to this popular wisdom of Chile—also present in other countries—God is on the side of the poor and at the last judgment the poor will have the last word.

In the twenties and thirties of this century, in the face of the adoration given by official Catholicism to Christ the King, some Catholic workers' organisations, led by Clotario Blest, raised the symbol of Jesus the Worker. And when violations of human rights occur under the military regime, there are many reformulations of old traditions which acquire an inevitable prophetic and protesting power in the light of events. The traditional popular pilgrimages to cemeteries on All Saints Day, for example, acquire a character of public protest when in the Santiago General Cemetery there are hundreds of tombs marked N.N. meaning those who were arrested, disappeared and were murdered by the secret police. Thus non-violent protest and religious protest are combined on innumerable occasions: Days of Prayer and Fasting for the Disappeared, Days for the 'Defence of Life', non-violent meetings against torture, religious funerals of the victims of repression in various circumstances, 'via crucis' of Popular Christian Communities etc. And in community life even the smallest signs e.g. the reading of a gospel passage, acquire a 'subversive' power towards the dominant order. Slowly a popular cult is developing towards the new martyrs from among the Christian people: Juan Alsina and Andre Jarlan, among many others.

This is a people, which, as well as being Christian, is also conscious of its situation and organising to fight for the defence of their rights, which have been taken away. Here we see a previously unknown alliance between the protesting power of popular religion and the prophetic and liberating dimension of official Christianity.

6. RELIGION AS SYMBOLIC PROTEST AGAINST OPPRESSION

We have considered different forms of protest latent in popular religion. Various ritual and representational expressions are in fact forms through which 'those below', the oppressed, distance themselves from the dominant culture and establish a principle of otherness and identity. Following Gramsci[7] we can say that many popular religious expressions contain an implicit view of the world in opposition (an opposition which is also often implicit, mechanical, objective) to the 'official' world view. However in every case this must be seen in its own historical and structural context.

Often symbolic protest is manifested in an *underground form*. The people, who have undergone a traumatic series of experiences of humiliation and oppression, protest covertly, without allowing their protests to come to the ears of the dominant power, in order to avoid annihilating reprisals. Therefore they often appear to be deprived of a voice. They are silent because they have been silenced but not because they are dumb.

This is a protest which makes it possible to survive to reconstruct a meaningful world through an attitude to life which it is difficult to reduce to rationalist formulae, and which gives a collective identity to popular culture. This is the people's way of defending itself on the symbolic plane against the viciously destructive oppression to which it is subject on the material plane.

Of course for the moment this form of latent protest serves the interests of the dominators. But this should not make us forget that it is in effect the 'sigh of the oppressed', 'protest against real wretchedness' (Marx).

Historical practice and the influence of a critical culture—mediated by organic intellectuals, clerical and lay—are what can make this protest become open and conscious. In this way popular religion becomes popular liberating Christianity, as we have seen in the recent historical experience of Latin America.

Translated by Dinah Livingstone

Notes

1. See Karl Marx 'Contribution to the Critique of Hegel's Philosophy of Law', in Karl Marx and Frederick Engels *Collected Works* (London 1975), III at pp. 3–129. In his analysis of popular religiosity Weber also shows how this acts to domesticate and legitimate the dominant powers. See M. Weber *The Theory of Social and Economic Organisation* (Oxford 1947) 1 pp. 358 ff.

2 An interpretation systematised by A. Bentué in an interesting study on popular religion in Santiago, Chile. See 'Funciones y significado de un tipo de religiosidad al interior de una subcultura' in *Religiosidad y Fe en América Latina* (Santiago 1976) pp. 61–76.

3 . See G. Gimenez *Cultura Popular y Religión en el Anahuac* (Mexico 1978); D. Irarrazaval *Relgión del pobre y Liberación en Chimbote* (Lima 1975); T. Kudo *Práctica religiosa y Proyecto Histórico* II (Lima 1980); C. Parker, W. Barra, M.A. Recuero, P. Sahili *Rasgos de cultura popular en poblaciones de Pudahuel* (Santiago de Chile 1981).

4. See B. Smith *The Church and Politics in Chile* (Princeton N.J. 1982) pp. 283–355; C. Parker 'Christianismo y Movimiento Popular en Chile' *Plural* 4 (1985) 9–36.

5. Although apt in many aspects, P. Bourdieu's theory of the religious field is insufficient in its analysis of the religious 'consumption' of the popular masses. See 'Genèse et structure du champ religieux' *Rev. fr. de Soc.* 12 (1971) 295–334.

6. See M. Salinas 'La sabiduría campesina y popular chilena del siglo XIX' *Araucaria de Chile* 19 (1982) 81–96; M. Salinas 'Pensamiento religioso popular de Chile' *Páginas* IV/19 (1979).

7. See A. Gramsci *Letteratura e vita nazionale* (*Einaudi* Turin, 1954) p. 215.

Virgil Elizondo

Popular Religion as Support of Identity; A Pastoral-Psychological Case-Study Based on the Mexican American Experience in the USA

INTRODUCTION

THE MEXICAN American is one who through birth or acquired nationality is *a citizen of the U.S.A. while maintaining a deep Mexican heritage.* Today there are approximately 14,300,000 Mexican Americans in the U.S.A. and the number continues to increase daily. It is a highly complex socio-cultural group that is quite at home in the U.S.A. without ever fully assimilating the U.S.A. way of life. It is neither fully 'U.S.A.-American' nor fully 'Latin-American'. It lived in its present day geographical setting long before the U.S.A. migrated west and took over the Mexican territories. One of the key factors in the group identity, cohesiveness and continuity of the group is the persistence of its religious symbolism which we will explore briefly in this presentation.

1. FUNCTION OF RELIGIOUS SYMBOLS

The popular expressions of the faith *function in totally different ways for various peoples depending on their history and socio-cultural status.* For the dominant culture, the popular expressions of the faith will serve to legitimise their way of life as God's true way for humanity. They will tranquilise the moral conscience and blind people from seeing the injustices which exist in daily life. For a colonised/oppressed/dominated group, they are the ultimate resistance to the attempts of the dominant culture to destroy them as a distinct group either through annihilation or through absorption and total assimilation. They will maintain alive the sense of injustice to which the people are subjected in their daily lives.

By popular expressions of the faith I do not refer to the private or individual devotions of a few people but to the *ensemble of beliefs, rituals, ceremonies, devotions and prayers which are commonly practiced by the people at large.* It is my contention, which is beyond the scope of this paper to develop but which will be its point of departure, that those expressions of the faith which are celebrated voluntarily by the majority of the people, transmitted from generation to generation by the people themselves and which go on with the Church, without it or even in spite of it, express the *deepest identity of the people.*

They are the ultimate foundation of the people's innermost being and the common expression of the collective soul of the people. They are supremely meaningful for the people who celebrate them and meaningless to the outsider. To the people whose very life-source they are, no explanation is necessary, but to the casual or scientific spectator no explanation will ever express or communicate their true and full meaning. Without them, there might be associations of individuals bound together by common interest (e.g. the corporation, the State, etc . . .), but there will never be the experience of being a people.

It is within the context of the tradition of the group that one experiences both a sense of *selfhood* and a sense of *belonging.* Furthermore it is within the tradition that one remains in contact both with one's beginnings through the geneologies and the stories of origins and with one's ultimate end. We are born into them and within them we discover our full and ultimate being. I might enjoy and admire other traditions very much, but I will never be fully at home within them. No matter how much I get into them, I will always have a sense of being other.

From the very beginning, Christianity presented a very unique way of universalising peoples without destroying their localised identity. People would neither have to disappear through assimilation nor be segregated as inferior. The Christian message interwove with the local religious traditions so as to give the people a deeper sense of local identity (a sense of rootedness) while at the same time breaking down the psycho-sociological barriers that kept nationalities separate and apart from each other so as to allow for a truly universal fellowship (a sense of universality). In other words, it *affirmed rootedness while destroying ghettoishness.* Christianity changed peoples and cultures not by destroying them, but by re-interpreting their core rituals and myths through the foundational ritual and myth of Christianity. Thus, now a Jew could still be a faithful Jew and yet belong fully to the new universal fellowship and equally a Greek or a Roman could still be fully Greek or Roman and equally belong to the new universal group.

2. RELIGIOUS TRADITIONS OF THE AMERICAS

The beginning of the Americas introduces *two radically distinct image/ myth re-presentations* of the Christian tradition. The *U.S.A. was born as a secular enterprise* with a deep sense of religious mission. The native religions were eliminated and totally supplanted by a new type of religion Puritan moralism, Presbyterian righteousness and Methodist social consciousness coupled with deism and the spirit of rugged individualism to provide a sound basis for the new nationalism which would function as the core religion of the land. It was *quite different in Latin America* where the religion of the old world clashed with those of the new and in their efforts to up-root the native religions found themselves totally assumed into them. Iberian Catholicism with its emphasis on clerical rituals and the divinely established monarchical nature of all society conquered physically but itself *was absorbed by the pre-Colombian spiritualism* with its emphasis on the harmonious unity of opposing tensions: male and female, suffering and happiness, self-annihilation and transcendence, individual and group, sacred and profane. In the secular based culture of the United States, it is the one who succeeds materially who appears to be the upright and righteous person—the good and saintly. In the pre-Colombian/Iberian-Catholic *mestizo* based culture of Mexico it is the one who can endure all the opposing tensions of life and not lose his or her interior harmony who appears to be the upright and righteous one.

With the great Western expansion of the U.S.A. in the 1800's, *50% of northern Mexico was conquered* and taken over by the U.S.A. The Mexicans living in that vast region spanning a territory of over 3500 kilometers from California to Texas, suddenly became aliens in their own land . . . foreigners who never left home. Their entire way of life was despised. The Mexican mestizo was abhored as a mongrel who was good only for cheap labour. Efforts were instituted *to suppress everything Mexican: customs, language and Mexican Catholicism.* The fair-skinned, blond Mexicans who remained had the choice of assimilating totally to the White, Anglo-Saxon Protestant culture of the U.S.A. or being ostracised as an inferior human being. The dark-skinned had no choice! They were marked as an inferior race destined to be the servants of the white master race.

Today, social unrest and dire poverty force many people from Mexico to move to the former Mexican territories which politically are part of the U.S.A. Newcomers are harrassed by the immigration services of the U.S.A. as illegal intruders—a curious irony since it was the U.S.A. who originally entered this region illegally and stole it from Mexico. Yet the descendants of the original settlers of this region plus those who have immigrated continue to feel at home, to resist efforts of destruction through assimilation and to celebrate their legitimacy as a people.

3. MEXICAN AMERICAN RELIGIOUS SYMBOLS

The Mexican Americans living in that vast borderland between the U.S.A. and Mexico have *not only survived* as a unique people but *have even maintained good mental health* in spite of the countless insults and put-downs suffered throughout its history and even in the present moment of time.[1] Anyone who has suffered such a long history of segregation, degradation and exploitation should be a mental wreck.[2] Yet, in spite of their on-going suffering, not only are the numbers increasing, but in general they are prospering, joyful and healthy thanks to the profound faith of the people as lived and expressed through the common religious practices of the group. I could explore many of them,[3] but I will limit myself to what I consider to be the *three sets of related core expressions* which mark the ultimate ground, the perimeters and the final aspirations of the Mexican American people: *Guadalupe/Baptism*; *dust/water*; *crucifixion/the 'dead' ones*. They are the symbols in which the apparently destructive forces of life are assumed, transcended and united. In them, we experience the ultimate meaning and destiny of our life pilgrimage.

There is no greater and more persistent symbol of Mexican and Mexican American identity than devotion to *Our Lady of GUADALUPE*. Thousands visit her home at Tepeyac each day and she keeps re-appearing daily throughout the Americas in the spontaneous prayers and artistic expressions of the people. In her, the people experience acceptance, dignity, love and protection . . . they dare to affirm life even when all others deny them life. Since her apparition she has been the flag of all the great movements of independence, betterment and liberty.

Were it not for Our Lady of Guadalupe[4] there would be no Mexican or Mexican American people today. The great Mexican nations had been defeated by the Spanish invasion which came to a violent and bloody climax in 1521. The native peoples who had not been killed no longer wanted to live. Everything of value to them, including their gods, had been destroyed. Nothing was worth living for. With this colossal catastrophe, their entire past became irrelevant. New diseases appeared and together with the trauma of the collective death-wish of the people, the native population decreased enormously.

It was *in the brown Virgin of Guadalupe that Mexicanity was born* and through her that the people have survived and developed. At the very moment when the pre-Colombian world had come to a drastic end, a totally unsuspected irruption took place in 1531 when, in the ancient site of the goddess Tonanzin, a Mestizo woman appeared to announce a new era for 'all the inhabitants of this land'. Guadalupe provides the spark which will allow the people to arise out of the realm of death like the rising phoenix arising out of the ashes of the past—not just a return to the past but the emergence of a spectacular newness.[5] In sharp contrast to the total rupture with the past which was initiated by the conquest-evangelisation enterprise, Guadalupe provided the necessary *sense of continuity* which is basic to human existence. Since the apparition took place at Tepeyac, the long venerated site of the goddess Tonanzin, it put people in direct contact with their ancient past and in communion with their own foundational mythology. It validated their ancestry while initiating them into something new. The missioners had said their ancestors had been wrong and that the diabolical past had to be totally eradicated. But the lady who introduced herself as the mother of the true God was now appearing among them and asking that a *temple* be built on this sacred site. Out of their own past and in close continuity with it, something truly sacred was now emerging.

Furthermore, she was giving meaning to the present moment in several ways for she was promising them love, defence and protection. At a time when the people had experienced the abandonment of their gods, the mother of the true God was now offering them her personal intervention. At a time when new racial and ethnic divisions were emerging, she was offering the basis of a new unity as the mother of all the inhabitants of the land. At a time when the natives were being instructed and told what to do by the Spaniards, she chose a low class Indian to be her trusted messenger who was to instruct the Spaniards through the person of the bishop and tell them what to do.

Finally, she initiated and proclaimed the new era which was now beginning. Over her womb is the Aztec glyph for the centre of the universe. Thus she carries the force which will gradually build up the civilisation which will be neither a simple restoration of the past nor simply New Spain but the beginning of something new. The sign of flowers, which she provided as a sign of her authenticity, was for the Indian world the sign which guaranteed that the new life would truly flourish.

Thus in Guadalupe, the *ancient beginnings connect with the present moment and point to what is yet to come*! The broken pieces of their ancient numinous world are now re-pieced in a totally new way. Out of the chaos, a new world of ultimate meaning is now emerging. The phoenix had truly come forth not just as a powerful new life, but also as the *numinosum* which would allow them to once again experience the awe and reverence of the sacred—not a sacred which was foreign and opposed to them, but one which ultimately legitimised them in their innermost being—both collectively as a people and individually as persons.

The second great religious expression is the BAPTISM of infants. The Lady of Guadalupe had sent the Indian Juan Diego to the Church. The Indian world immediately started to go to church and ask for baptism. Yet, they were no longer being up-rooted totally from their ancient ways in order to enter into the Church which the Lady had sent them. They were entering as they were—with their customs, their rituals, their songs, their dances and their pilgrimages. The old Franciscan missioners feared this greatly. Many thought it was a devil's trick to subvert their missionary efforts. But the people kept on coming. They were truly building the new temple the Lady had requested: the living temple of Mexican Christians. It is through baptism that every new-born Mexican enters personally into the temple requested by the Lady. Through baptism the child becomes part of the continuum and is guaranteed life in spite of the social forces against life. The community claims the child as its very own and with pride presents it to the entire people. In the group, the child will receive great affirmation and tenderness. This will give the child a profound sense of existential security. He/she will be able to affirm selfhood in spite of the put-downs and insults of society: they will dare to be who they are—and they will be who they are with a great sense of pride!

The ASHES of the beginning of Lent are a curious and mysterious religious expression of the Mexican tradition which finds its full socio-religious meaning when coupled with the HOLY WATER which is blessed during the Easter Vigil. For people who have been forced to become foreigners in their own land, who have been driven from their properties and who have been pushed around by the powerful in the way the mighty wind blows the dust around, ashes, as a moment of the continuum of the pilgrimage of life, become most powerful. They mark the radical acceptance of the moment—actually there is no choice. But this is not the end for the people do not only come for ashes, throughout the year they come for *holy water* to sprinkle upon themselves, their children, their homes . . . everything. They are very aware that our entire world yearns and travails in pain awaiting to be redeemed—a redemption which in Christ has indeed begun but whose rehabilitating effects are yet to take effect in our world of present day injustices. The sprinkling with the waters of the Easter Vigil is a constant call for the *regeneration of all of creation.* The dust which is sprinkled with the water will be turned into fertile earth and produce in great abundance. As in the reception of ashes there is an acceptance, in the sprinkling of holy water there is an unquestioned affirmation: the ashes will again become earth: the dust-people will become the fertile earth and the earth will once again be ours. The *dust-water binomial* symbolises the great suffering of an up-rooted people who refuse to give in to despair but live in the unquestioned hope of the new life that is sure to come.

The final set of religious celebrations which express the core identity of the Mexican American people is the CRUCIFIXION which is celebrated on Good Friday, and THE DEAD whose day is celebrated on November 2. For a people who have consistently been subjected to injustice, cruelty and early death, the image of the crucified is the supreme symbol of life in spite of the multiple daily threats of death. If there was something good and redemptive in the unjust condemnation and crucifixion of the God-man, then, as senseless and useless as our suffering appears to be, there must be something of ultimate goodness and transcendent value in it. We don't understand it, but in Jesus the God-man who suffered for our salvation, we affirm it and in this very affirmation receive the power to endure it without it destroying us. *Even if we are killed, we cannot be destroyed.* This is the curious irony of our celebrations of the dead: they appear to be dead, but they are not really dead! For they live not only in God but in our hearts and in our memory. Those whom the world thinks are dead . . . those who have been killed by society . . . defy death and are alive in us. In our celebrations of memory, their presence is keenly experienced. Thus what is celebrated as the day of the dead is in effect the celebration of life—a life which not even death can destroy. Society might take our lands away, marginate us and even kill us, but it cannot destroy us. For we live on in the generations to come and in them we continue to be alive.

CONCLUSION

The *conquest of ancient Mexico by Spain in 1521* and then the *conquest of northwest Mexico by the United States in the 1840's* forced the native population and their succeeding generations into a split and meaningless existence. It was a mortal collective catastrophe of gigantic death-bearing consequences. Yet the people have survived as a people through the *emergence of new religious symbols* and the re-interpretation of old ones which have connected the past with the present and projected into the future. The core religious expressions as celebrated and transmitted by the people are the unifying symbols in which the opposing forces of life are brought together into a harmonious tension so as to give the people who participate in them the experience of *wholeness*. In them and through them, opposites are brought together and push towards a resolution and the people who celebrate them experience an overcoming of the split. Where formerly there was opposition, now there is reconciliation and even greater yet, synthesis. This is precisely what gives joy and meaning to life, indeed makes life possible in any meaningful sense regardless of the situation: and it is in the celebration of these festivals of being and memory that the people live on as a people.

Notes

1. R. Acuña *Occupied America* (San Francisco 1972)

2. Roberto Jiminez 'Social Changes/Emotional Health' in Medical Gazette of South Texas 7 No 25 (20 June 1985)

3 For a greater discussion of other religious symbols, consult my previous works: *Christianity and Culture* and *La Morenita, Evangelizar of The Americas* (San Antonio); *Galilean Journey, The Mexican American Promise* (New York: 1983).

4 For other aspects of Guadalupe, consult my previous articles in *Concilium* 102 (1977) and 168 (1983).

5 J. Ruffie *De La Biologie A La Culture* (Paris: 1976) pp 247-252.

Sidbe Semporé

Popular Religion in Africa: Benin as a Typical Instance

> In order to understand a religion, *pace* our doctors in
> theology, whether lay or clerical, popular beliefs are much
> more important than refined, abstract forms.

C. Hainchelin *Les Origines de la religion*

BLACK AFRICA is a privileged place for the flowering and vitality of
popular religiosity. The religions that originate elsewhere, principally Islam
and Christianity, have willy nilly to take account of this inescapable reality
that impregnates and tropicalises practice and belief. The case of Benin, the
former region of Dahomey, is in this respect enlightening and instructive.

A small country counting a little less than four million inhabitants, situated
on the South-West coast of Africa, what used to be Dahomey is famous not
only by reason of the town of Ouidah, the capital of the centuries-long traffic
in slaves; not only by reason of the town of Abomey, centre of an original
kingdom and symbol of a fierce resistance to French occupation at the end of
the nineteenth century; but also on account of its religious traditions, which
were the sources and direct inspiration of the voodooism of Haiti and the
candombles of Brazil.[1] The Christianisation of the country, undertaken from
1861 onwards by Catholic missionaries, followed at the turn of the twentieth
century by Protestant preachers, was at first restricted to the Southern regions
and there found its points of support in the centres of Porto Nuovo, Cotonou,
Ouidah and Allada. This goes to explain why it is that today more than 90 per
cent of the 600,000 Catholics are concentrated in the southern third of the
country. The dominant languages and traditions of this Catholic population
are Fon and Yoruba.

1. CHRISTIANITY REAPPROPRIATED

Limiting ourselves to the examination of Fon and Yoruba Christianity, we have to conclude that this Christianity is exploding in all directions under the internal pressure of the ferment of religiosity left by a tradition that is more alive than ever. What we have is, on the one hand, *received* Christianity with all its dogmas, moral code and its cult transmitted and guaranteed by the hierarchy and its helpers of every degree; on the other hand, *lived* Christianity as it is apprehended by the mass of the people and assimilated according to the mental schemas and affective channels that have been pre-established and pre-determined by tradition and terrain. Let us confine ourselves to getting our bearings in this process of reappropriation in matters where faith makes decisive choices: the conception the Benin Christian has of *God*, his or her relation to *Jesus Christ*, her or his vision of what it is *to be human* and what *human destiny* is about.

(a) Christian God or Just God?

One can ask oneself what the Benin Christian is thinking about when he refers to God by the names Mawu, Sè or Olorun. The definitions he or she learned so labouriously from the catechism will certainly be in his or her memory. But her or his God will more likely be the product of the blending between the God of the Bible, the God of the missionaries and the God of the Ancestors. Deeming it a sort of indiscretion or indecency as he or she does to 'dig into' the mystery of the Being-beyond-understanding, he or she is content to say that He *is*, that is to say, that He is Life; that He *brings things about*, that is to say that He brings existence about; that He *reigns*, that is to say, that He ensures retribution. The dogmatic assertions of official religion about the unicity, the immutability and the paternity of God are substantially nuanced and reinterpreted by popular belief and practice.

They will, of course, confess 'one sole God', but what is in question is, not a unicity of exclusion, as theology teaches, but a *unicity of inclusion* opening out into a plurality of modes of existence on the part of God. Without necessarily referring to the Fon or Yoruba pantheon of Ancestors who surrounded the Great Being with indispensable associates, the ordinary Christian in Benin finds himself or herself naturally attuned to the Christian dogma of the Trinity reinterpreted as the affirmation of a plural deity. For the Christian in the street they are three Gods who make only one, and a modest inquiry among young people about their idea of God and of the Trinity reveals that they move in an ambience of a distinctly associationist or subordination-ist conception of the Trinity.

As for the immovable and eternal God, his only interest is the fact that he just is not treated like that in the minds of those who, on the contrary, love to immerse him deeply in time. If God is *before* all, he is nevertheless not outside time, and his *eternity* is only an *anteriority* that is incommensurable *within time*. The image of the ageless Old Man fits this temporal God perfectly. On the other hand, he is not thought of as immovable, because immovability can in no way characterise the living, and in such popular thinking the adage 'Vita est in motu', 'Life consists in movement' is self-evident. God, like any living being, changes and reacts in accordance with circumstances and times. The only things that are characterised as immovable are the customs and laws of society.

Finally, God is invoked and recognised as *Father*, not so much in the sense of the one who establishes links of intimacy and reciprocity with human beings but rather in the sense of the one who grounds and maintains existence. In Fon, for example, the term 'T ' signifies at once 'Father' (or genitor) and 'owner' (or master). The Father is the *paterfamilias*, the head of the family who establishes the family hearth and guarantees the continuity of the lign. The child recognises and affirms the paternity of the Father by keeping his distance and his respect, by maintaining gratitude and submission, all of them attitudes that Christians take over spontaneously in regard to God the Father and Master. The God of the creed, 'all powerful Father', meets with the assent of the Benin Christian who venerates him rather as the Source and Master of life than as a partner in intimate and familiar relationships.

(b) Jesus Christ, Tutelary Hero

At the heart of the Christian faith Jesus Christ for the mass of Benin Christians takes on the figure of a protective Hero, a sort of Titan and advocate for human beings. Son of God in good fortune, son of Adam in ill, Jesus remains in popular imagination and piety as it were a Prometheus who wanted to console human beings and improve the human condition, for which he was tortured and eliminated by the forces of Evil at work in the world. In the final analysis his defeat speaks more loudly than his victory.

The parts of his earthly activity that are retained the most are the thaumaturgic 'works' rather than the evangelical teachings that supports them. For Christians ceaselessly confronted with problems of sickness, famine and witchcraft, the miracles of healing, multiplication (of bread and wine) and exorcism are enough to fix the personality of Jesus and to characterise his mission. This is the Jesus who attracts and arrests, this is the one they invoke and wait upon.

There is, however, also the other Jesus, the one humiliated and tortured.

This Jesus, the victim of the conjoint malice of human beings and occult Forces, focuses popular sympathy and piety in a quite special way. What happens in effect in the heart of the Christian is a sort of secret identification between his or her actually being a target and a victim and the Man of Calvary. The Risen one galvanises people much less than the Crucified one, and the celebration of Good Friday and of the way of the cross in Benin has a great popular success that denotes a distinct displacement of accent compared with the official liturgy. The man of sorrows fascinates people by his wounds, his blood, his crown of thorns, his falls, his isolation, his being crushed, his cross, and above all, his calumniated innocence and his despised resignation. Without going so far as to burn Judas the traitor in effigy, as the Blacks used to do in Peru, Christians in Benin are no less indignant at the role he played in the tragic end of the Master, as well as at the attitude of Him who, deaf to tears and entreaty, let things take their course—and the vehemence of their feelings is sometimes scarcely contained. For people who think like this, the Resurrection seems to amount, at best, to catching up somewhat too late. Delivered up by the Father and by Judas, Jesus knew in advance that his destiny was sealed and his cause was heard.

In everyday life relationship to Jesus is before all else affective and cultic, it is in no way cerebral. The 'christic' devotions that flourish here and there in Cotonou, Porto Nuovo and elsewhere and which are addressed to the Little Infant of Prague, the Holy Face, the Sacred Heart, etc. correspond more to the strong need for group association than to any deliberate desire for confessional proselytising. As for the Eucharist, it is perceived as the Bread of Heaven, and it is received as a mysterious remedy for the ills of existence. The holy fear it inspires, and that goes some way to explain why it is expressly forbidden to receive communion in the hand, arises from the hidden forces the consecrated substance is thought to hide. Communion with the sacred Bread is essentially a participation in these mysterious forces rather than a making present once again of the Paschal mystery, or a mystical union with Christ and his Body. The priest, through whom this mysterious transmutation of elements into Medications is effected, is in Benin thought of as being invested with redoubtable powers and forces.

Half-God, half-man, Jesus for the mass of Christians in Benin remains a tutelary Hero, a 'Vodun' who is unique in the qualities he has and supreme in the efficacy he deploys.[2]

(c) Human Beings and their Destiny

The spontaneous and constant reaction of the Benin Christian faced with human destiny contradicts the Christian postulate of a happiness desired for all by God. While admitting the evangelical principle of salvation proffered to all at the theoretical level, he or she has the gut conviction that each human person has his or her star and trajectory determined by the Creator from before his or her birth. This is what gives rise to the inevitable question of predestination that surfaces regularly in study and prayer groups, and that is summarily resolved by submission—tranquil or anguished—to the 'will of God'. The Benin Christian links up spontaneously with Semitic thinking and is quite ready to affirm with Ben Sirach: 'Good things and bad, life and death, poverty and wealth, come from the Lord' (Sirach 11:14). Human destiny and freedom seem to be terribly overlaid by a nexus of supra-human forces and influences directing and regulating her or his life.

At the same time the Christian lives his resignation actively, by putting in motion a certain number of means calculated to influence the course of his or her destiny or the will of the Master of destinies in her or his favour.

In the first place, he or she deploys every means to pierce the veil of destiny, to discern the factors that preside over the course of her or his life. Recourse to *consultation*, deeply rooted in ancestral customs, persists and develops under the Christian regime. We here find ourselves in the presence of a phenomenon rooted in what I want to call a *fatic* mentality[3] according to which one consults about everything: birth and death, healing and dying. Depending on the circumstances, the Benin Christian will have recourse to the following for a consultation: despite the formal prohibition of the hierarchy, a good number of the faithful confide their interrogations and anguishes to the *traditional diviner*. Others prefer to resort to *visionaries* of the famous Benin Church of 'Celestial Christianity' who rely on prayer in the Spirit to penetrate the secrets of existence.[4] Others yet again search hither and thither within the Catholic Church for *seers* or *messengers*.

In Cotonou thousands of Christians have been going for many years now to pray to and consult 'the Sacred Face' in the home of an old Christian woman who responds to consultations.

In Porto Novo a young woman has over the past years kept people talking by drawing crowds through phenomena of bleeding and clairvoyance.

In Cotonou, since 1984, a cult of Padre Pio has developed round a 'messenger' and with the blessing of the hierarchy. This expresses the need to 'consult' and to regulate one's life in accordance with revelations, oracles and the messages of seers confirmed by popular acclaim.

Popular Christianity also tries to loosen the grip of destiny by resorting to 'armour plating', that is to say by making use of *sacred means of protection* against sinister devices and influences. Here too the Christian can either adopt—even in bad conscience—the panoply of charms, amulets and other fetishes bequeathed by the ancestors—or content himself or herself with carrying, employing or burying in his or her own home Christian 'fetishes' recognised for their efficacy—holy water, ashes, blessed palms, miraculous medals, *agnus dei*, images, crucifixes, rosaries, relics . . . .

In a world where belief in sorcerers and their redoubtable wiles is widespread it is hardly surprising to meet among Christians such a need for security and such an enthusiasm for sensible objects of protection without which they would feel naked and vulnerable.

Besides the means of protection that form as it were a covering against the harmfulness and malignity of the environment, the Christian also disposes of *means of pressure* which she or he uses in season and out of season in order to seize favours, obtain support or negotiate a situation. Prayer is thought of above all as a way of putting pressure on God and on the saints. This explains the hectic recourse to 'infallible', 'miraculous' 'strong' prayers, in the first rank of which one has to put the 'psalms'. These prayers that formerly were consigned to the priest's breviary are for this reason considered to be invested with quasi-magical powers and efficacy. Every day people come to ask us for the 'key to the psalms' in order to learn to use them on their own behalf against enemies. People also have recourse to prayers and chains of prayers the codified recitation of which ensures miraculous results, so it is thought. This is the way in which in Cotonou, Porto Novo, and elsewhere the 'efficacious' prayers of St Charlemagne, St Bridget, St Anthony, St Jude, Father Julio etc circulate. Amongst the most redoubtable of such prayers are to be counted chains of prayers which, assorted as they are with threatening clauses, are executed, multiplied and ventilated with fear and trembling. Ascetic or penitential practices like fasts, stations of the cross, novenas and pilgrimages are, most of the time, calculated to 'soften' the heart of God or even to force his hand, like the importunate friend in Luke 11:4 ff.

Finally, the sentiment that human beings realise their destiny best only in the midst of group that carries and nourishes them leads the Christian to be a member of one or more *associations*. Just as in traditional society human beings live and realise themselves only by belonging to the social group, the Christian seeks support, protection and recognition at the heart of associations where she or he can feel themselves taken care of.

The parish community as such is too vast and too anonymous to respond to the desire for joint living and mutual aid that animates the Christian. This is why there are so many associations, to the point that they can number up to forty within the boundaries of a single parish. They bear names such as the following:

Our Lady of the Sacred Heart, Our Lady of Montligeon, Little Infant Jesus of Prague, Militia of Jesus Christ, Padre Pio, Tarcisius, Charles de Foucauld, Emmanuel, etc. On the principle that two securities are worth more than one, many people become members of many associations, whether they are expressly recognized as Catholic, or whether they have been denounced as esoteric, like the Rosicrucians, Eckhankar, the Mahikari ... or pagan, like Gouro or Mamy Wata. In any case Benin Christianity, like African or Black-American Christianity is tending to become a Christianity of *brotherhoods*, in the medieval or Islamic sense of that word.

2. GOD WILL RECOGNISE HIS OWN

At the end of this brief survey of certain aspects of popular religion in Benin, I am tempted to go beyond what I have reported and to suggest that pastors and theologians often find themselves at odds with the actual life of faith as it is expressed among the mass of the believers. Sadolet is right to make Erasmus say: 'Not that it is not much more right to fix all one's attention on Christ; yet these popular cults are not alien to our faith as long as everybody cannot easily raise themselves to the height of Christocentric meditation.' And the fathers of the most recent Synod in Rome (November/December 1985) are saying nothing else when they affirm: 'Popular devotions, properly understood and correctly practised, are very useful for feeding the holiness of the people. This is why they deserve more attention from pastors' (Official Report II A 4).

The invitation to take popular religion seriously is first of all an invitation to get to know it, and not only in its manifestations and fruits but above all in its motivation and roots. Too often, however, people are content to take a superficial look that canonises or condemns on the basis of prefabricated criteria or schemas.

In Africa, Africanisation is all the rage, inculturation understood in the sense of a task reserved in fact for theological or pastoral specialists. The result, a product of sundry injections, applications or grafts of cultural elements that have sometimes been rather too hastily indexed, has hardly gone beyond the stage of facile accommodation that is very far from touching the deeper layers of being. Now what people are too superior to acknowledge is that the Africanisation of Christianity has *already* been partly *realised*, and that at the root of being where one forges existence in the crucible of aspiration, hope and fear, the rude faith of simple people has ended up by producing a Christianity that is profoundly African, and potentially evangelical. Whether one blushes or rejoices about it, this Christianity of the masses embodies an authentic African response to the Gospel understood and lived in the cultural and religious context of yesterday and today. It is not a matter of assuming an air of condescending surprise at the weaknesses and limits of such a Christianity, in the way in which a missionary once did vis-a-vis the Aymaras Indians: 'And one thought they were Christian!'[5] Nor does it do to say that Benin Christians are after all Christians like any other Christians. What is at issue is to face the facts: Africanisation or inculturation does not come about as a result of plans preconceived from on high but as a result of what is lived at the base. It is true that this popular Christianity is the work of the little and the lowly (Matt. 11:25), of that 'rabble who do not know the law' (John 7:49), and that as such it is called to a constant conversion and purification in living response to the Gospel. Its practices and beliefs are not exempt from impurities and deviations, far from it. But one would gain far more if one were not to assume straight away that it is a gross patois or an upsetting perversion, but rather to sit down in the dust on the same ground as this mass Christianity in order to discover its originality and to allow oneself to be convinced that even here God knows how to recognise his own.

Translated by John London

Notes

1. The Voodoo of Haiti is the prolongation, albeit in a syncretist form, of the Dahomey cult of the 'Vodun' as it has been transposed into a Christian milieu. The Brazilian *candombles*, especially those of Bahia, are the result of a blend of several African cults, and particularly those of the Yoruba and the Fon of Nigeria and of ancient Dahomey.
2. The 'Vodun' are protective and beneficent divinities among the Fon.
3. I here bring together the 'fatum' of the ancient Romans and Greeks and the 'Fa' of the Fon people, which are agencies and instruments of divination. The 'Fa' are consulted and the diviner throws the 'Fa' in order to decipher the invisible and to interpret events. Consulting the 'Fa' (or Ifa among the Yoruba) is tantamount to seeking to align oneself with or withdraw from the constraints of fate.
4. For the place of 'consultation' and the role of visionaries in the Church of Celestial Christianity, I take the liberty of referring readers to my study of Afro-Christian churches in *Lumière et Vie* 159, 43–59.
5. The title of a well-known book by Père J.E. Monast.

Rosemary Radford Ruether

Women-Church: Emerging Feminist Liturgical Communities

TO SPEAK of *popular religion in a feminist context* may seem surprising to many people. Popular or 'folk' religion is usually thought of as arising among peasant peoples, often representing as syncreticism of Christianity and pre-Christian survivals. It is thought of as a spontaneous expression of less literate groups in society who make their own amalgamation of official Christianity and ancient cultural practices which serve the popular needs of daily life. This does not fit the model of feminist popular liturgical communities which are part of a conscious movement growing out of theological and historical criticism of patriarchal influence on Christian theology and ministry.

Women, since the early days of Christianity, have been thought of as a docile and conservative population who attend church in larger numbers than males and can be counted on to accept practices taught them by the clergy. For *women to form separate 'conventicles'* (other than religious orders) is unknown in the history of the Church, even among sectarian groups. Whatever protest women may have felt against male domination in earlier periods of Christian history, this criticism has been contained within larger movements of protest. One example is the Society of Friends in the seventeenth-century English Reformation where women leaders, such as Margaret Fell, argued for the equality of women and men in teaching and church leadership. Polytheistic religions have sometimes had special cults or rites that pertained only to women, but this was within a larger complementarity of male and female religious expressions of one ethnic and cultural community.

52

Thus for women to form female-centered protest gatherings for worship, theological reflection and ministry is unprecedented.

It is not possible to tell at this point whether this movement will become established as an organisation, or whether those participating in such groups will grow in numbers sufficiently to make real impact on existing religious cultures, even if only by the significant withdrawal of female participation in regular churches. The movement may dissipate or its creative work be re-absorbed into established historical churches. But whatever its future, feminist liturgical gatherings have grown sufficiently in the last decade, particularly in the United States, but also in Western Europe, to be at least worthy of note.

Feminist liturgical communities represent the *growing alienation of feminist women* (and some men) from the patriarchal paradigm of Christian (and Jewish) religion. For thousands of years males (of the ruling classes) have claimed a *monopoly on the imaging and representation of God* and have excluded women from ministry, preaching and theological education (at the university level). This means not only that women have not participated in these leadership roles, but also that the entire patterning of Christianity has been one in which male domination over women has been the model for divine transcendency over the human. Women are seen as representing the creaturely both in the negative sense of that which alienates us from God (sexuality and sin) and also in the positive sense of passive receptivity to divine action. But, in neither sense can women represent God or God's representative in Christ.

For about one hundred and thirty-five years there has been *a struggle within Protestantism for ordained status for women*. This struggle opened ordained ministry to some Protestant women in the nineteenth century (Congregationalists, Unitarians, Universalists and a few others), but mainstream Protestant churches in the United States (Presbyterian, Methodist) did not change their policy on this until 1956. Lutherans, Episcopalians and other Protestants have voted to include women in ordained ministry in the 1960's and 70's. Women began to attend Protestant and even Catholic seminaries in growing numbers in the 1970's and also to attain the rank of theological professor as well. This allowed, for the first time, the possibility of the *systematic exploration of sexist bias* in theological tradition. Women began to ask not only for practical inclusion in leadership but for a systematic critique and transformation of those theological teachings and religious images which had been shaped by the millenia of exclusion of women.

Women, however, quickly experienced the *resistance* of both the theological schools and the churches to these questions. Where women could be ordained they were seldom given real authority. Efforts to open up theological language and imagery created hostile reaction. Even when denominational leadership attempted to be responsive, conservative forces in the churches and the general culture were negative. For example, the National Council of Churches of Christ in the U.S.A. commissioned an *Inclusive Language Lectionary* to be written. Male and female scholars, both theologians and biblical exegetes, studied the traditional lectionary readings in the original languages and sought gender inclusive language. They also revised some of the selections of readings, dropping passages such as Ephesians 5 which enjoins the wife to be subject to her husband (the parallel text of Ephesians 6, 5-9, telling slaves to obey their masters was dropped from the lectionary in the 1920's).

This effort generated not only a storm of hostile protest and outright rejection from many Church leaders and lay Christians, but there were even threats against the lives of those who worked on the lectionary committee. Most women who had become concerned about these issues did not experience anything so dramatic as a death threat. But most experienced such resistance to their efforts to obtain even the most minimal changes that they began to *despair of the established churches* as places capable of responding to feminist questions. The more they became feminists the harder it became to go to church. Those who felt most in need of religious nurture to support their growing sense of personhood began to look for other *alternatives*. They began to create free space to shape language and liturgical action that could express women's anger and pain and celebrate women's new potential. It became apparent that what such women were seeking was not simply a minor tinkering with details of dress, grammar and personnel of worship, but a whole new religious culture.

Not surprisingly, it has been *Roman Catholic women* who have a strong liturgical tradition, but who also have felt *most blocked* by the hierarchical leadership from even the most minor participation in ministry or changes in language, who have been at the forefront of what has come to be called '*the women-church movement*'. In the United States this movement has grown out of the temporary abandonment of the cause of women's ordination. In 1975 some sixteen hundred Roman Catholic women (ninety percent nuns) gathered in Detroit for the first national meeting for women's ordination. The conference gave birth to the *Women's Ordination Conference*, a national organisation which defined its goals as two-fold, both the winning of ordained priesthood for Roman Catholic women and the renewal of priestly ministry itself. These Roman Catholic women never saw themselves as wishing to be included in priestly ministry defined in its present clerical mode, but sought a priesthood renewed in service to the people as part of their own quest to be included in ordained ministry.

However, by the 1980's, an *increasingly reactionary papacy* was not only hostile to any new questions of women's ministry, but was seeking to turn back those expressions of collegiality and reform that had taken place under the inspiration of the Second Vatican Council. The repression of women in the church was a major aspect of this reactionary movement led by the Vatican. Democratised women's religious orders were told to restore traditional patterns of authority. Seminaries were ordered to remove women from roles of pastoral counselling to seminarians. Even the most minor participation of women in roles of altar servers was rejected by Rome. Accordingly, Roman Catholic women began to *put the question of ordination aside* and concentrate instead on a renewed practice for ministering and worshipping community.

In 1983 the remnants of the Women's Ordination Conference, together with a number of other grass-roots Catholic women's organisations, representing both nuns and lay women, came together as the *Women of the Church Coalition*. They planned a conference to explore this change of direction, called *Woman Church Speaks* (the change to 'Women' took place later in order to express the plurality of women across class, race and culture). The conference (which was bilingual in English and Spanish and made a major effort to provide scholarships for poor women) modelled the agenda of women's vision of Church as a *community of liberation of women from patriarchy*. The conference was attended by more than twelve thousand women, almost all Roman Catholics, forty percent nuns and sixty percent lay women. This was a dramatic shift from the ordination conference of eight years earlier and demonstrated the movement toward real coalition-building between nuns and lay women. Some of these lay women were ex-nuns, but many represented a new development of theologically educated lay women.

The Chicago conference was *primarily liturgical in character*. All the mass meetings took place in a context of liturgical song, dance and ritual, so that the plenary speakers were 'preachers' rather than lecturers. In addition to the mass gatherings, there were also *many small workshops* clustered around the three themes of 'spirituality', 'sexuality' and 'survival'. Under 'spirituality' there were workshops on feminist theology, counselling and retreat work and particularly the development of feminist liturgies and liturgical communities. Under 'sexuality' were considered such topics as sexual life style, celibacy, marriage, divorced women, lesbians, single women, reproductive rights, rape, incest, pornography and prostitution. Under 'survival' were such topics as women with children poor and alone, women on welfare, violence toward women, ageing women, women refugees, women church workers, militarism, unemployment, and finally, organising and networking for social change.

After the conference the planning groups decided that they wanted to remain as *distinct organisations* with different constituencies among Catholic women, but to work together as a *coalition* to form a national network to support both the idea of women-church and to empower grass-roots communities. It was decided that any local group of women with as many as three members ('where two or three are gathered together') could call themselves a women-church group and could become a member of the national network, but that there could be no individual membership. In effect, the women-church movement has become a network for promoting *feminist base communities*. Women-church groups model themselves partly on base communities in the Latin American church that combine elements of prayer, theological reflection and worship with transformational social practice. But they recontextualise this concept in terms of the liberation of women from patriarchal oppression, both by society and by the church.

There seem to be *two major types* of feminist liturgical communities. One type takes the form of a *small intentional community* that meets at least weekly and creates liturgies that express the ongoing spiritual journey of the community. Responsibility for developing the liturgy is passed around among the members and may be followed by intense discussion of the meaning of the liturgy. A second type is organised on a *city-wide basis* by a sponsoring organisation, such as Chicago Catholic Women in Chicago or the Feminist Theological Center in Boston. Although there may be rotation among those who plan the liturgy, there is still a distinction between the planning and sponsoring group and those who come to 'attend' it. Such larger liturgies take place more occasionally, such as monthly. Some who participate either in the first or the second type of feminist liturgy may also attend official masses as well. For others, this is their sole worshipping community. But generally such gatherings are seen as *ecclesiolae in ecclesia*, not as efforts to found a new historical church. Feminist liturgies also take place as special gatherings, such as conferences on feminist theology, or meetings of women church workers.

Such gatherings display a *freedom to reshape all traditional elements of worship*. While biblical texts may be used with feminist commentary, feminist poetry or prose may also become 'text'. In one conference on feminist liturgies in Washington, D.C., attended by some two hundred persons, the 'Parable of the Naked Lady' (a feminist parable written in the style of a gospel parable) was acted out by a mime troop. (For this parable, see R. Ruether *Womanguides: Texts for Feminist Theology* [Boston: Beacon Press, 1985, pp.

248–251].) The conference and its liturgies was developed by WATER (Women's Alliance for Theology, Ethics and Ritual), a group that regularly organises such conferences.

Traditional eucharistic elements, such as blessing and sharing bread and wine may be used, but also other eucharistic elements such as milk and honey, or apples. Other traditional rites, such as baptism or exorcism may be adapted to feminist meaning. Baptismal signing of each other with water becomes a symbol of rebirth from patriarchy. One may ceremonially 'exorcise' women from the evil power of patriarchal theology and Scripture. Any existing thing may become a sacramental symbol when imbued with new meaning as a part of liberation from alienation and oppression.

Although many who have been actively involved in such liturgical gatherings have been of Roman Catholic background, there is typically a sense of *ecumenical outreach*, not only throughout the Christian tradition, but including the Jewish tradition as well. Elements from Jewish tradition, such as Passover and Sabbath meals, have been integrated into feminist liturgies. Such liturgies in the Jewish tradition allow worship to take place around an actual common meal. Feminists have also been engaged in developing *rites for new occasions typically neglected by the patriarchal traditions*, such as healing rites for physical and sexual abuse of women, healing after an abortion or a miscarriage, ending liturgies after divorce or in leaving a religious order and transitions to new stages of life. Moments in women's life cycle, such as puberty or menopause may be lifted up as times of ritual celebration. Such liturgies not only express the positive possibilities of such transitions, but also heal from the feelings of guilt, shame, or simply anonymity imposed on those who have no way of articulating in community critical moments in their lives.

Most of these liturgical communities are not also communities of social practice directly. But the women involved in feminist liturgy are also, typically, involved in issues of *social justice*, both for feminist causes, such as reproductive rights or violence to women, and issues of peace and justice against nuclear armaments, American intervention in Central America or apartheid in South Africa. Thus there is a strong interconnection between feminist liturgical communities and liberation social praxis.

The women-church movement among Christian feminists in paralleled by somewhat similar movements among *Jewish feminists*. Jewish women began to gain entry into rabbinical education in the 1960's in the United States and have been ordained in the Reform and Reconstructionist traditions for some time. Only recently, they have also been accepted in the Conservative tradition. The Orthodox tradition still rejects ordination for women and denies women certain areas of study and prayer reserved for men. Traditionally, women were not counted in the *minyan* (minimum of ten required for communal prayer). Since Jewish women were traditionally excluded not only from the rabbinate, but even from adult lay participation, the first struggle of Jewish religious feminists has been to struggle for full inclusion in prayer and study. But it also became apparent that key ceremonies of initiation, such as circumcision as the rite of incorporation into the covenant of Israel and the *bar mitzvah*, had no female counterparts. Jewish women had to ask, in a even more basic way than Christian women, whether they were really even included in the historical covenant of their community.

One response has been to create *parallel liturgies for girls*, a ceremony of initiation of a female baby into the covenant, and *bat mitzvah*, or rite of entrance of a thirteen-year-old girl into adult status in the community. Orthodox women took the initiative in forming women's *minyan* or female assemblies for communal prayer. These developments were part of a larger movement of liturgical renewal among American Jews who sought to renew a more *communal and justice-oriented Jewish religious practice.* Arthur Waskow, once a secular political activist who turned to Jewish religious renewal in the 1960's and is now a professor of the Reconstructionist seminary in Philadelphia, has been a leader in this kind of *Havurah* movement among religious Jews interested in uniting their religion with concerns for gender equality, economic justice and preventing nuclear holocaust.

Waskow has focused particularly on imaginative ways of reconnecting Jewish religious life style with social commitment. Serious observance of the Sabbath comes to be understood as a resistance to a work and profit-oriented economy and a focus on the true 'ends' of human life in harmonious being with God and creation. Keeping kosher becomes a way of avoiding the foods and products produced by oppressive systems of exploitation of land and labour. The whole cycle of the yearly holidays becomes a way of connecting with aspects of protest against injustice and anticipating God's true Shalom of peace and justice, culminating in Passover as the great feast of liberation from slavery. This kind of renewed Judaism lends itself very readily to *dialogue and interrelationships with liberation types of Christianity.*

Some women of Jewish and Christian background have concluded that these *traditions cannot include women fully.* They believe that patriarchal religions, such as Judiasm and Christianity, have as their fundament *raison d'être* the sacralisation of male domination. They see biblical patriarchy as having arisen in antiquity as part of the overthrow of earlier female-centered religions and societies, and they believe that feminist spirituality should focus on *reviving these ancient Goddess religions*, rather than trying to reform patriarchal religion. This viewpoint often appeals to women who come from the most conservative wings of Judaism and Christianity, who have been socialised to feel deep needs for ritual and religious nurture, but despair of meeting those needs in their own religious traditions.

The *'Wicca' religion*, as it is sometimes called, takes the form of small communities (covens or gatherings of thirteen) who observe rituals based on the planetary cycles of the winter and summer solstices and the vernal and autumnal equinoxes. Other rituals connect with moments in women's life cycle: conception, birth, first menstruation, menopause, croning (become a wise old woman). Other rites are intended to gather power to protest against or exorcise evil and draw benefits (love or wealth) to oneself. Much of this kind of Goddess or neo-pagan feminism thinks of ritual as magic. They see such magic as efficacious spiritual power for making changes in the world.

The *relations between Jewish and Christian feminists and neo-pagan feminists* are highly ambivalent. Implicit, if not explicit, in neo-pagan feminism is a total rejection of positive content for women in biblical faith. At most, such Goddess feminists look on Jewish and Christian feminists as only partly 'liberated'. Some Jewish feminists look on such neo-pagans as exemplars of that idolatry condemned by the very foundations of Jewish faith, whereas others see it more as the older foundations of a semitic religious tradition out of which Judaism itself emerged. It is not uncommon among gatherings of Jewish feminists to have both options represented. Both Jewish and Christian women might also ask critical questions about the presumed accuracy of the neo-pagan 'myth' of primitive matriarchy and gynecentric religion that preceded patriarchy. On a more theological level, one might ask whether there is, in religion based on nature-cycles, an *adequate anthropology that can ground a responsible ethic.*

Discussion on such questions on a meaningful level has not been possible between these movements because of the emotional feelings on both sides. But what one does typically see in practice is a kind of *practical ecumenism and electicism*, in which all of these options might be present in a conference on feminist spirituality sponsored by chaplancies of universities. Christian feminist women, while not adopting the Wicca perspective *in toto*, nevertheless might find particular ritual ideas useable, such as solstice or life-cycle rites. Perhaps, as these movements continue to coexist and come to trust each other more, it may become possible to enter into deeper discussion on differences and to discover whether these differences are fundamental or whether they represent *different pieces in a larger vision* of a world redeemed from violence and injustice and integrated in a harmonious way into the nexus of renewed creation.

Part II

Theological Perspectives on Popular Religion

Hermann Vorländer

Aspects of Popular Religion In The Old Testament

IT IS only in recent times that the popular religion of Israel has been made the subject of research, after long being dismissed, under the influence of dialectical theology, as primitive and non-Jahwistic.[1] In what follows, the term 'popular religion' refers to the popular ideas entertained by the Israelites concerning God's action in the life of the individual, the community, and in nature. To a large extent they shared these ideas with the neighbouring peoples. Popular religion was by no means exclusively centred on Jahwe until the Exile; it presupposed the existence of several divinities. In this regard there can be no hard and fast distinction between Canaanite and Israelite religion. Belief in Jahwe, with its monotheistic thrust, only crystallised out after centuries of confrontation with the popular religion. Initially what we have is a multifarious religious life, where, besides the official worship of Jahwe, the God of the State and the nation, there were still numerous private and local cults.

Characteristic of Israelite popular religion is its close connection with the needs and experiences of everyday life. Vestiges of this in the Old Testament were largely obliterated by later, official theology and have to be painstakingly reconstituted (hypothetically, in part). The material for this task is provided by polemical texts, old legends, popular stories, prayers and personal names.

INDIVIDUAL PIETY

We begin with an example from personal life, the story of Jacob's dream-revelation in Bethel (Gen. 28:10–22). Jacob had to leave his father's house because he had deceived his elder brother. Now he is without protection, as regards both his family and his family god. He then receives a startling experience of God during the night. He is given the promise that God will give him the land and bless him with many descendants. Next morning, having become aware, in numinous awe, of the holiness of the place, he erects a stone as a visible sign of the divine presence, making a vow: 'If God will be with me, and will keep me in this way that I go, and will give me bread to eat and clothing to wear, so that I come again to my father's house in peace, then the Lord shall be my God' (v. 20f). This vow characteristically reflects the expectations a man had of his god: his presence should provide protection, nourishment and clothing, and ensure a safe return. Only when Jacob has tested the power of his god, will he bind himself to him for ever. The following chapters tell how this comes about: God makes Jacob's father in law, Laban, rich for his sake (Gen. 30:27). When differences arise between Jacob and Laban, Jacob's God does not allow Laban to harm him (Gen. 31:7). Then the two men make a covenant, in which each swears by the name of his family god (Gen. 31:48–54). Jacob returns home a prosperous man and is reconciled to his brother (Gen. 32f). In a solemn vow he dedicates himself and his family to the God who appeared to him in Bethel (Gen. 35:1–7).

The kind of personal piety we find in Jacob and the other patriarchs is addressed to the type of personal God who can be shown to be venerated throughout the popular religion of the ancient East. The individual knows that he and his family are bound to one divinity, among all the numerous gods, in a specially intimate way. Through his presence, the personal god gives health, success, the blessing of children, good relations with fellow men, and protects him against evil powers and evil men. Thus a life of fulfilment testifies to the influence of the personal god.

Genesis 28 speaks of an ancient holy place, which was probably marked by a prominent stone. As well as stones, other places signify a special divine nearness in popular religion, e.g., mountains, rivers or trees (See Exod. 3; Gen. 32:23ff; Judg. 6:11). The erection of the stone is intended to facilitate a permanent relationship to the god through the cult. In the cult, man receives the renewing, protecting and blessing power he needs for his life, but also for the maintenance of the social order. The gift of the tithe expresses the fact that Jacob owes all that he has to God and in this way gives a portion of it back to him.

The biblical tradition also traces the success of other important figures back to the direct action of God, e.g., in the case of Joseph (see Gen. 39:2–5) or David (see 1 Sam. 16:18; 2 Sam. 5:10). What is true of these men, applies *mutatis mutandis* to every biography. According to the folk-tale account of Gen. 2:7, God breathed the breath of life into the first man. This process is repeated at every birth: God draws the human being from the mother's womb (Pss. 22:10; 71:6). He can also close up the womb (1 Sam. 1:5) and cause barrenness (Gen. 20:18). Life is felt to be something miraculous, inexplicable, depending directly on God.

Human life is continually threatened by hostile powers. Psalm 22 describes how these exert their influence. The speaker is a sick man, his body is dried up, his strength is gone, he suffers pains all over his body (v. 14f). Evidently he holds demons responsible for this attack of sickness, for he compares them to wild beasts (vv. 13, 16). Belief in demons played a bigger part in the popular religion of Israel than our present Old Testament would suggest. In a few places we find magic and witchcraft explicitly forbidden (Ezek. 13:18; Jer. 27:9). The demons Resheph (Hab. 3:5[Heb]) and Lilith (Isa. 34:14[Heb]) are mentioned by name, as well as the spirits of the open places (2 Kings 23:8). We must suppose that many cultic prescriptions originate in ritual protection against demons. Evil spirits create illnesses, e.g., in the case of Saul (1 Sam. 16:14) as well as political errors of judgment, e.g., David's decision to count the people (2 Sam. 24:1) or Rehoboam's obstinacy (1 Kings 12:15).

Demonic powers can only exercise influence on the author of Psalm 22 because his God turned away from him. Thus, full of bitterness, he complains that his God has left him (v. 2). The consequence of this is that his fellow men also turn against him, and he becomes a laughing-stock (vv. 7–9). They accuse him of not being in a right relationship with God and point to his fate as evidence of this. Israelite popular religion makes a close connection between what a person does and what happens to him, between one's attitude and one's fate in life. 'By his actions man "creates" a permanent envelope around him that brings him good or ill fortune.'[2] A happy life points to God being with the person concerned; thus the psalmist's enemies deduce from his illness that his relationship to God has been upset by sin. However, he refuses to give up hoping in his personal God and pleads for his life to be renewed. To die prematurely would be bad, for the popular view is that only a long life is a fulfilled life.

In Israelite folk-religion human life is traced directly to God's action. We must be clear about the fundamental meaning of the Hebrew word for God, *el* or *elohim*. Originally it may have had something to do with 'power, strength' and can thus be compared with the concept of *mana* which is well known to the history of religions.[3] When man encounters the divine, he encounters a power that is able to bring good or evil. Often this power seems puzzling and violent to him. So, by means of cult, sacrifice, prayer and right conduct, he seeks to placate the threatening divine presence and attract its positive energies. The popular religion of Israel and its neighbours had no theoretical interest in God-in-himself; it was concerned with the practical ways and means of encouraging God's nearness and assistance.

The question of the existence of divine beings did not arise. Only a fool could deny it (Ps. 10:4). The only reservation was whether God's action was detectable in a particular situation. In Old Testament spirituality the experience of God and the understanding of reality formed an indivisible unity. Man experienced God's dealings everywhere in the reality that surrounded him. In these ancient texts we are confronted with a unitary understanding of the world that traces everything, this-worldly and other-worldly, natural and supernatural, internal and external, to a single, divinely-created order.

EXPERIENCE OF GOD IN NATURE

God's action was discerned not only in personal life but also in nature. The absence of vegetation indicated God's anger (see Amos 4:6–9).During a period of drought Jahwe appeared to the people like a stranger or a traveller (Jer. 14:8), unable effectively to control natural events. The whole of nature was experienced as a miraculous spectacle, maintained by God. Since people had no concept of natural laws, they thought of miracles in terms of extraordinary manifestations of divine power. Miracles were not so much felt as 'unnatural', but as rare occurrences, which did not suspend the regularity of natural events. They were seen as indications of God's power, without which nature could not continue (see Gen. 8:20–22).

Many festivals were originally nature festivals, serving to maintain both the vitality of nature and the life of the community. Thus, at the Feast of Weeks, the firstfruits of the crops were offered. By giving this tribute of the firstfruits man acknowledged that God was the giver of growth and increase. Only after he had returned to God part of the harvest, could he use the rest for himself (see Exod. 23:16). Furthermore, the Feast of Booths was originally a harvest festival which was celebrated after the vintage. Later the feasts were 'historicised' and thus detached from the cycle of nature.

POPULAR RELIGION AND FAITH IN JAHWE

Originally Jahwe had no particularly close relation to nature; he was only associated with weather, lightning, thunder and clouds (see Exod. 19:7-19; Deut. 33:26). For a long time many Israelites were much closer to the local gods of Palestine than to the Jahwe who came out of the desert. The Old Testament does not conceal the fact that these gods were intensively venerated. Thus Jer. 11:13 complains that the Israelites had as many gods as they had cities. Often they are lumped together as Baals and Ashtaroth and represented as mere fertility gods (see Judg. 2:13f etc.). But in fact they also served as local divinities (see Amos 8:14) and were venerated privately (see Jer. 7:18; 44:15ff). As elsewhere in the ancient Near East, Israelite personal names reflect individual piety. Thus in the Old Testament we often find Baal- names borne not only by ordinary people, but even by members of the King's household (see 2 Sam. 4:4; 1 Kings 4:12). Archaeology has brought to light numerous figurines of divinities, as well as inscriptions with Baal- names, in Israelite towns.[4]

Crucial for the triumph of faith in Jahwe was the fact that David chose Jahwe as the personal God of his dynasty and so raised him to the rank of a State god. His successor, Solomon, built the Temple in Jerusalem, which served both as a private shrine and as a State temple. Together with the royal House of David it was particularly Jewish upper class which, in addition to the official cult, practised personal veneration of Jahwe. Thus the cult of Jahwe was more firmly rooted in Juda than in the Northern Kingdom of Israel, and it intensified towards the end of the period of the monarchy. This is indicated by the increase in the proportion of Jahwe-names, as archaeology demonstrates.

Even the official cult of Jahwe was permeated by elements of popular religion right into the time of the monarchy. Its character was not yet monotheistic or exclusive. Otherwise it would be impossible to understand how there was an *ashera* even in the Jerusalem Temple (see 2 Kings 21:7). Furthermore, the Temple was built on an ancient Jebusite cultic location (cf. 2 Sam. 24). There are many indications that Solomon simply renovated and extended the existing shrine. Jahwe was primarily venerated in Israel as the God of the King and the people, similarly to Chemosh among the Moabites. This is expressed in what Jephtha says to the enemy king in Judg. 11:24: 'Will you not possess what Chemosh your god gives you to possess? And all that the Lord our God has dispossessed before us, we will possess.' Jahwe and the Moabite god Chemosh provide victory for the peoples under their respective protection. In popular religion it was evidently El who was venerated as the chief god. We know of him from Ugarit, as the creator and king of gods and men. In its original text Deut. 32:8f contains a strange reference to El, who gave Israel to Jahwe as his inheritance. This is substantiated by the striking fact that the Old Testament nowhere attacks or criticises El.

At the centre of the national cult stood the temple. It was held to be the source of life for the people and the place of safety (Jer. 7:10; Hag. 1f.). It was here that David had brought the Ark, an ancient cultic symbol for the presence of Jahwe, which went back to Israel's nomadic past. Every (male) Israelite was obliged to participate in the national cult (Exod. 23:17). If a person left the community of the nation, he also left his ancestral religion (see. 1 Sam 26:19). In the temple the priests mediated the nearness and the blessing of God by performing prayers, sacrifices and rituals.

In popular belief the king was very close to God; in 1 Kings 21:10,13 he is spoken of in the same breath. By his anointing he was endowed with special power and dignity, and so could not be touched (see 1 Sam. 24:7,11). The king exercised certain priestly functions and mediated divine blessing to the people (1 Kings 8). He was regarded as the 'breath of life' of his people (Lam. 4:20). His wars were Jahwe's wars (see Josh. 10:10ff.). In God's place he guaranteed law and order, without which community life was impossible. In the destiny of his kingship Israel experienced the beneficent presence and fateful absence of the king's God.

The religion of ancient Israel thus presents us with a very varied picture. The different levels of the official religion of Jahwe, the local cults, and individual piety existed side by side. This picture is confirmed by the discoveries of Elephantine. The Jewish military colony which lived there, in Upper Egypt, was probably founded by the Persians in the 6th century B.C. The texts found there have brought astonishing facts to light: while these Jews worshipped Jahwe as their chief God, a certain part was also played by a divine triad consisting of Asham-Bethel, Anat-Bethel and Haram-Bethel. They swore by the name of Jahwe, but also invoked Egyptian and Babylonian gods. At the centre was a temple of Jahwe, yet they were by no means monotheists. Naturally, this archaeological discovery must be evaluated cautiously; but we are no doubt justified in following the opinion of E. Meyer[5] that the situation in Elephantine is typical of Judaic popular religion prior to the Exile.

POPULAR RELIGION: CRITIQUE AND INTEGRATION

Even before the Exile, the prophets destroyed the popular belief in the abiding and natural connection between Jahwe and his people. Amos is the first to proclaim that Jahwe has terminated his relationshp with Israel because of its sins and is about to visit his judgment upon it (Amos 8:2). Micah contradicts the accepted view that Jahwe must maintain his temple at all costs (Mic. 3:9–12). Hosea compares the worship of alien gods, common in the popular religion, to adultery, which must be punished accordingly (Hos. 1 and 3). The decisive break with popular religion did not take place, however, until the Exile. Those exiled could not take the many cult-objects of their local gods with them to Babylon. Conversely, the cult of Jahwe was easier to transplant since in all probability it was essentially hostile to images. Furthermore, Babylon lacked the holy places where people had been wont to worship their gods; and the exiles belonged mainly to the upper class, which—as we have seen—was more committed to faith in Jahwe than the rest of the population. But not only popular religion was now in deep crisis: faith in Jahwe was too. Many Israelites came to doubt the power of Jahwe to assert himself against other gods. Clearly, he had forsaken his people (see Ezek. 8:12), so the only course was to turn to the Babylonian gods (see Jer. 16:13).

The prophet Deutero-Isaiah responds to this national and religious crisis by proclaiming Jahwe as the only and universal God. In the catastrophe of 586 B.C. Jahwe has demonstrated, not his lack of power, but his power to judge and bring salvation. Furthermore he has taken over the function of the Creator-God, El (see Isa. 40:12ff). All other gods are nothing and cannot influence history and events (Isa. 41:11,24). Deutero-Isaiah was less concerned, however, to condemn idolatry than to stress the total availability and nearness of Jahwe. The Israelites no longer need the alien gods because they can look to Jahwe for everything. He is as personally near to them as the local gods were hitherto. He cares for them and will carry them 'even to old age' (Isa. 46:4). Consequently the prophet addresses Israel in personal terms and calls Jahwe 'my God' (Isa. 40:27; 49:14). Even the belief in demonic powers is no longer necessary to explain evil, for it is Jahwe who creates 'weal and woe' (Isa. 45:7).

In a similar way the Deuteronomist theology emphasises Jahwe's personal involvement: 'For what great nation is there that has a god so near to it as the Lord our God is to us, whenever we call upon him?' (Deut. 4:7) Jahwe cares like a father for all the personal needs of the Israelites, including their baskets of meal. He keeps sickness far from them and gives the rain (Deut. 7:12ff; 28:1ff.). Here, however, there is severe condemnation for the cult of alien gods and magical practices.

By being integrated into the popular religion, faith in Jahwe acquired a personal dimension which was hitherto practically unknown to Israelites on the basis of the official cult of Jahwe. Since Jahwe was the sole God, he had to take on both functions: that of the sublime ruler of the world, and that of the familiar god. At many points this tension proved too strong. Jahwe retreated more and more to an unattainable remoteness and partly lost contact with everyday life. So, after the Exile, elements of popular religion once more acquire importance. The figure of Satan now comes to embody evil (see Job 1:6); angels appear as intermediaries between God and man (see Dan. 12:1). This shows that the dialogue with popular religion continues after the Exile.

Faith in Jahwe arose on the foundation of Israelite popular religion and developed in a critical dialogue with it. We can only understand its distinctive character against this background. Popular religion emphasises the aspect of nearness to human existence by closely linking the experience of God and the experiences of life. Faith in Jahwe becomes remote from life, theoretical, unless it is continually enriched by the influence of popular religion.

Translated by Graham Harrison

Notes

1. See Martin Rose *Der Ausschliesslichkeitsanspruch Jahwes. Deuteronomische Schultheologie und die Volksfrömmigkeit in der späten Königszeit* (Stuttgart 1975) BWANT 106; Rainer Albertz *Persönliche Frömmigkeit und offizielle Religion. Religionsinterner Pluralismus in Israel und Babylon* (Stuttgart 1978) CTM A,9; Hermann Vorländer *Mein Gott. Die Vorstellungen vom persönlichen Gott im Alten Orient und im Alten Testament* (Kevelaer and Neukirchen 1975) ADAT 23.
2. Klaus Koch 'Gibt es ein Vergeltungsdogma im Alten Testament?' ZThK 52 (1955) 1–42, 31.
3. See Werner H. Schmidt's article 'el. Gott' in *Theologisches Handwörterbuch zum Alten Testament* (Munich 1971) 142–149.
4. See the work by Rose cited in note 1, at pp. 171ff.
5. *Der Papyrusfund von Elephantine* (Leipzig ³1912) 40.

Ernest Henau

Popular Religiosity and Christian Faith

ONE OF the distinctive features of our present way of thinking is that we *evaluate popular religiosity positively*. In a culture that was strongly influenced by the rationalism of the Enlightenment and by nineteenth-century progressive thinking, there was apparently no room for a certain kind of religiosity and this was consequently dismissed as an outdated form of superstition and magic that had its origin in a mythical and already superseded view of reality. Within the Church itself, certain developments, connected with the practice of going back to the biblical sources, led to the growth in the liturgical and ecumenical movement of a critical attitude towards many different forms of traditional piety.

The *overwhelming majority of theologians* and most of those responsible for pastoral care had *little or no appreciation of the positive value of popular piety*. They also took no notice of the data provided by research in other theological disciplines in which some interest was taken in the phenomenon of popular religiosity. The sociologist Serge Bonnet therefore felt impelled to change his style of writing and become a pamphleteer, comparing himself to a cowboy thrusting violently into the bar of the 'Ecclesiastical City' because no one listened to him outside and shooting at the ceiling.[1]

The *tide was turning*, however, and from 1973 onwards very many books and articles devoted to this subject have appeared. One only has to glance at these publications to recognise that popular religiosity has been defined in many different ways. The various ways of looking at the subject have led to a wide variety of emphases and definitions, in many of which attention is drawn to only one element. A more historical and anthropological approach is favoured by L. Maldonado, who defines popular religion as 'lived' religiosity, in contrast to 'official' or 'prescribed' religiosity.[2] A. Vergote, on the other hand, favours a psychological approach, which leads him to regard 'habit' as the most characteristic element in popular Catholicism.[3] Following A. Gramsci, Italian authors have simply equated popular religiosity with 'folk-lore' or else have described it as an 'expression of a wrong consciousness', imposed on the proletariat by the ruling class.[4]

Although descriptions of this kind are to some extent quite legitimate, they do easily lead to a kind of *reductionism*. The only way of avoiding this danger is to try to find a *more general definition* able to embrace the whole spectrum of popular religious phenomena and to indicate the basis that they have in common.

An analysis of the *noun 'people'* and its derivatives may, I think, lead us to this better definition. With this word it is possible to describe a group of people who form a whole on the basis of a common language, culture, history (and possibly even structure of the State). In a tradition that can be traced back to the Romantic movement, this description has a positive significance, because it includes an intact intuition, a creative power and a deep sense of the divine.

Sometimes the word 'popular' derives its meaning from a tradition that goes back to the Enlightenment, in which case it indicates *only a part of that whole*—the great mass of economically less privileged people with elementary school education who are guided by their feelings rather than by their reason, who need external signs for their religious experience and who are not capable of a mature faith. What is particularly striking here is that 'people' is defined in the light of a deficiency of something (education, power, influence and so on). What is lacking is the possession of a small group (the ruling class, an élite, intellectuals and so on).

This analysis points clearly to the fact that popular religiosity has to be understood in the widest possible sense. All the same, if the word 'people' is understood with this second meaning in mind, that is, as a part of the whole, what has to be recognised is that it is a part in which something special is lacking. Seen against this background, then, it is legitimate to regard popular religiosity as coinciding to a very great extent with religiosity as such, in other words, with being universally involved with the divine.[5]

The universality of the various forms of popular piety is a strong point in favour of this identification, since these forms have archetypal roots and are found beyond the frontiers of the concrete religions. This claim is further strengthened by the fact that certain historians are of the opinion that what we have in some forms of popular religiosity is simply a partly Christianised religiosity and even very early, pagan and naturalistic forms of religion that are present in Christian clothing within the Church.

The views defended some years ago by the *philosopher of religion B. Welte* also lend support to the claim that popular religiosity to a very great extent coincides with universal religiosity. Welte took as his point of departure the hypothesis that modern culture and society exist as it were simultaneously at two levels—at a higher, conscious, autonomous and rational level that is open to the whole world and also at an unconscious, suppressed level, which is the level at which religion is situated.[6] Fundamental to Welte's theory is the presupposition that this primitive world of man with its essential religiosity has not ceased to exist. In support of his hypothesis, he regards certain phenomena in contemporary culture as signals of a primary and original consciousness. One of these signals is popular religiosity, which, he believes, has to be regarded in this perspective as an expression of universal religiosity, that is, an involvement with the divine.

In this sense, the *social psychologist R. Towler* prefers the word 'common' to the term 'popular religion', because, in his opinion, all religions form a 'baseline of general experience' that is specified by the institutional expression of the religion in question.[7]

1. POPULAR RELIGIOSITY AND CHRISTIAN FAITH

This brings us to the problem of the *relationship between religion and Christian faith*, a problem that is still dominated by the views of *Karl Barth* and *Dietrich Bonhoeffer*. According to Barth, revelation can, if it is taken quite seriously, only mean one thing—the sovereign act of God's grace, in which God communicates himself and makes himself known to us. In Barth's view, then, religion is simply unbelief. It is not an authentic answer to God's manifestation of himself in Christ. All religions appear as attempts at self-justification and self-redemption. Revelation exposes these attempts and discloses their non-necessity, that is, the innate impotence of man to bring about truth. Conceived as religion, even Christianity is unbelief. We can only accept it as the true religion if we make an act of faith, but it does not require this qualification in its concrete form.

Barth's view is based on an enormous respect for the *sovereignty of God*, but it is quite legitimate to question the opening chapters of his exegesis of Paul's Epistle to the Romans on which this view is based. What is more, the monolithic way in which Barth states the problem does not leave room for the possibility of placing the positive significance and the grandiose nature of religions in the light, even though he recognises these factors. Finally, it should be pointed out that he added considerable light and shade to his views later, although he did not in fact change their fundamental orientation in any way.

The situation is a little more difficult to understand in the case of *Bonhoeffer*. It is highly likely that he was originally deeply influenced by Barth and gave the concept of religion a theological content. It is, however, possible to detect a *change of emphasis* in his *Letters and Papers from Prison*, in which he gives 'religion' a cultural and historical meaning and refers to a mode of religiosity in which God only has a place within a marginal experience of human shortcomings that becomes increasingly smaller. It is a religion of the 'hereafter' and interiority, which, in Bonhoeffer's opinion, is played out. But this is not a bad thing, since the God of the Bible is quite a different God. He is a God who is present as a redeeming force in the concrete history of man and who is manifest not in omnipotence, but in the weakness and the suffering of Christ.

It is obvious that what we have in Barth's work is a concept of religion which is powerfully historically determined (see Schleiermacher's liberal theology) and in which religion is seen as a cultural expression and therefore as a human product. Turning to Bonhoeffer, on the other hand, we find to some extent specific expressions and forms of piety that played a definite part in his own life and even more importantly an image of God that forms an intrinsic part of a certain religiosity. What is very significant in the theology of both Barth and Bonhoeffer, however, is that the *word 'religion' has a negative overtone* and that all forms of religiosity—including all popular religion—are seen as ambiguous. In this respect, the attitude of both these Protestant theologians can to some extent be contrasted with the *view predominating in Catholic theology*, in which religion and faith are not seen to be in dialectical tension with each other or as putting an end to each other, but rather as a direct extension of each other.

For my part, I would certainly defend the position that the relationship between religion and faith should not be defined as a discontinuity and that *religion is a positive aspect* or an indispensable stage on the way to the formation of the Christian sense of the sacred.[8] I regard religion as a relatively independent aspect within Christian faith and therefore believe that popular religiosity can be seen as a legitimate contextualisation of our experience of

God. (This does not mean that it is a perfect contextualisation of that experience.)

Paul's preaching to the people of Lystra (Acts (Acts 14:8–20) and more especially his address on the Areopagus (Acts 17:22–31) provide support for the idea that religion is a positive aspect of Christian faith. The apostle takes the statues of the Greek deities as his tactical point of departure and attempts to find reasons for persuading the Greeks to recognise the God of Jesus Christ as the 'unknown God', whose altar he had seen in Athens: 'What therefore you worship as unknown, this I proclaim to you'. It would be doing violence to Paul (or to the author of Acts) to regard this tactical position simply and solely as a rhetorical trick used by a clever orator. Paul would not have been able to speak in this way if there had been a complete break between the religion and the philosophy of the Greeks on the one hand and Christian faith on the other.

The *early Christians* certainly did not recognise such a radical break. Justin (100–165 A.D.), for example, affirmed that, although Christianity was undoubtedly the only true religion, there were germs of the 'logos' present and active in all men. Clement of Alexandria (150–215 A.D.) acknowledged the presence of divine teaching in the various ways by which men came to God.

This theory became so to speak a basic theological concept, embracing as it did a means of clarifying what God intended to do with the great variety of religious attitudes that prevailed among mankind. It is also possible to include within this framework the *incorporation of many pagan practices and habits into the Christian liturgy and Christian praxis.* This process of incorporation has formed an integral part of the Christian ethos, at least since the time of Gregory the Great, who insisted in his instruction to Augustine of Canterbury that everything that was not directly in conflict with the Gospel should be retained.[9] There are many other examples of this practice, including Nicholas of Cusa's ideas concerning what is common to all religions, Matteo Ricci's views on the Chinese rites and practices and the teaching of the Enlightenment about natural religion. Finally, it is worth recalling the distinction made at the First Vatican Council between man's knowledge of God on the basis of his being created and his knowledge of God on the basis of the Christian revelation. What the Council had to say about knowledge can be logically extended to include the relationship between God and man in general.

It should therefore be clear from this that religion and faith are not mutually exclusive, but are rather *two different realities that do not necessarily coincide.* This means that we have to be on our guard against two dangers. On the one hand, there is a risk of *extreme exclusivism*, in which no positive significance of any kind is attributed to religion and, on the other, there is an equal risk of a kind of *spiritual imperialism*, in which all forms of religion are annexed by Christian faith. (The theory of 'anonymous Christianity' is exposed to the second risk.)

A distinction should therefore always be preserved between *religion and faith*, with a consequent dialectical tension between the two. It is only on the basis of this distinction that it is possible to evole a kind of criteriology by means of which we should be able to avoid accepting anything as a legitimate expression of Christian faith. Revelation and its own special rationality can in this way be preserved as a critical principle by means of which aberrant and distorted forms as such may be given recognition. In the context of the problem that we are considering here, the tension between religion and faith can be seen to exist at the following levels. Firstly, there is the problematical division between the profane and the sacral. Secondly, there is the tension between personal salvation and the 'political' dimension of Christian faith. Thirdly, there is the relationship between the symbol and symbolised reality. Fourthly, there is the interaction between practice and the personal option and finally there is the tension between feeling and reason.

2. THE AMBIVALENCE OF POPULAR RELIGIOSITY

(a) *Holy places* play a very important part in popular religion, but Christianity has done away with the division between the profane and the sacral. God's sanctifying power is, according to Christian teaching, in principle universal because of his complete solidarity with man and the whole of creation in Jesus Christ. There are therefore no special places where his power is manifested in preference to other places. This is already quite clear in the Old Testament and especially in the prophetic tradition, which is extended into the New Testament. *Neither God nor the sacral are tied to a numinous place.* God has to be worshipped in spirit and in truth, because he is himself the only temple (see Rev 21:22).

This does not mean that the distinction between the profane and the sacral is insignificant. It only means that it can no longer be used in order to divide reality into two different spheres. The point of departure, then, is no longer the separation of the profane from the sacral, but the *essential interrelationship* between them. Through his revelation, God is closely related to man without any degree of relativity, without being removed in any respect from time and without being present simply within man's individual existence. His relationship with man takes place, on the contrary, within man's history and in the world. It is precisely for this reason that Christian faith needs images and symbols which point to the divine reality and which as such have a special significance and are charged with a special meaning.

(b) *R. Schreiter* has pointed out that popular religiosity is characterised among other things by a special way of looking at the world as a place where *everything is interconnected and checked.*[10] Every wrong action in punished and every good action is rewarded, because God sees everything. Because of this interconnection and checking, man has only very restricted space in which to manoeuvre. This leads in many cases to a certain fatalism with regard to the possibility of man taking the initiative.

The experience of popular religion is also dominated by man's needs of the moment, which are always very concrete. This is reflected, for example, in *popular prayer*, which only takes two forms: petition and thanksgiving. Gratuitous praise hardly ever finds a place in popular prayer. This frequently gives rise to a *very privatised form of religiosity* that is closely related to self. Religion is, of course, always concerned with the individual and his needs, but an exclusive concentration on this reduces the impact both of the concept of the Kingdom of God as a society living in justice and peace and the idea of the communal nature of faith. In addition, this form of religiosity can also have an alienating effect, because it closes the individual's eyes to the structures of society that can enslave him and prevents him from taking control of his own destiny and from looking for the best ways of changing this situation. On the other hand, however, certain forms of popular religiosity also contain an element of protest and express man's longing for a world that is not dominated by suffering and pain. They therefore have a strong utopian potential.

(c) *'Mediations'* are important in popular religiosity. These include, for example, blessings, relics, medals, rosaries, statues and holy pictures, candles, holy water and ashes. Association with such mediations can, of course, easily lead to *magic*: 'This may occur when symbols, in which the presence of God and his saving power is manifested, are turned upside down. When this happens, they no longer function as symbols on the basis and by virtue of what is symbolised, but are used in order to regulate the presence of God and his saving power and to compel them to be present. When Christians associate with symbols, this is not so much because man wants to manipulate God by means of them, but rather because he wants to let himself be manipulated. In so far as religiosity is an approach to God, making him subordinate to the human measure—this was Karl Barth's great suspicion—then it has to be rejected'.[11]

In concrete cases, there is, however, a great need for *caution. H. Biezais* had good reasons for disputing the fundamental separation made between faith and magic and for defending the view that any attempt to insist on such a separation is based on an ideology which gives an absolute value to one's own religion and religious experience.[12]

Even if we regard Biezais' assertion as somewhat obscure, it is still important to grasp the essential truth contained in what he is saying. R. Schreiter has, for example, pointed to the fundamental analogy between the lighting of a candle by a poor married couple who want to achieve a better relationship in their marriage on the one hand and the taking part in a 'marriage encounter' weekend by an educated couple who want to improve the communicative quality of their marriage on the other.[13] If we take as our point of departure the fact that association with symbols and 'mediations' in popular religion has by definition to be considered as magic, then we are bound to disregard the magical elements that are encountered even in the more enlightened forms of religious experience and we shall also *fail to take into account the positive aspect that is present in the experience of popular religiosity*, including, for example, an indisputable trust in God. In addition, we shall also not be aware of the need for a mediation by the senses, without which not only religion but also faith are impossible: *per visibilia ad invisibilia*.

(d) Seen from one point of view, popular religiosity is also a *collection of rites and practices*, in which the emphasis is above all on the carrying out of those practices without too much reflection. Popular religion is therefore based not so much on a personal option as on an experience of plausibility.

Faith, on the other hand, is an *extremely personal act* based on freedom and presupposing conversion and a change of heart. It cannot do without rites and practices, but there is always a risk that it may become insubstantial and be merged into the mere carrying out of ritual actions or the performance of familiar practices. In that case, those rites and practices become themselves the content of Christian faith and lose their character as means of conveying faith.

These considerations should not, however, make us lose sight of the *positive aspect concealed within a religion of religious practices*. Both individuals and communities feel that those practices form a link with their own past and help them to situate themselves in a meaningful history of successive generations. Their awareness of being *embedded in a valuable tradition* gives them a sense of identity, certainty and security. The world that they live in is threatened with chaos and full of harsh contrasts and those religious practices enable them to feel part of a meaningful and stable order. Rites, customs and practices that are taken over in this way do not have to be in themselves empty or inauthentic. A practice can become one's own practice! Practices may, on the other hand, be taken over and accepted and rites may be performed because one has learned to do this and it has always been the case. When that happens, the custom is preserved because it expresses a way of life to which one gives one's full consent and which one regards as valuable, even though one may not be able to formulate its value as a theme.

(e) There can be no doubt that *feeling predominates in popular religiosity*. This may, of course, lead to an opposition to reason and, if that happens, aberrant forms of religiosity will sooner or later inevitably appear. This does not necessarily mean that *rationality is the only criterion* by which religious expressions may be judged, nor does it mean that rationality is able to prevent every form of distortion. Feeling and reason can be critical of and can correct each other. Faith is never pure feeling. If it were, it would no longer be possible to make a coherent confession of faith, preaching would be reduced to glossolalia and Christians would no longer be able to be 'called to account for the hope that is in them' (1 Pet. 3:15). There is also a very real danger that partial aspects of faith may be given an absolute value if there is no regulating authority and this can always lead to fanaticism and polarisation. On the other hand, a religion from which all elements of feeling have been eliminated will be narrowed down to a collection of abstract pronouncements. If Christian faith is examined closely, it always shows itself to be an *embodied truth* that has in fact always been transmitted and experienced much more in the form of stories, presentation and role play than in definitions and logical argument.

It is in this assertion that we have to look for the origin of the often tense relationship between *theology and popular religiosity*. The latter is religion which is lived and experienced, which is not expressed in formulae and which is transmitted by means of other forms. It leads to insights and intuitions which cannot be adequately contained within the framework of formulated logic and which can therefore easily be dismissed as subjective and emotive.

On the other hand, the 'people' often see the theologian as a pedant or a 'spoil-sport', as someone, in other words, who has a low opinion of what is simple. That is, of course, a wrong judgment, since faith is in itself, that is, as an attitude or an expression of one's existence, fundamentally simple, whereas the precise verbal expression of faith cannot be simple. It is always difficult to *express in words why we believe* and the essence of our attitude as believers, but it is a task that has to be undertaken again and again. It has to be done in the light of our conviction that it is necessary to move away from abstraction and return to concrete human experience, in other words, to 'simple faith' and its modes of expression. This is not an uncommitted task, but one that forms an essential part of our search for the truth of faith.

3. CONCLUSION

Every attempt that we make to *define the reality of God* in concepts or to grasp it imaginatively or figuratively is bound to fail. This conviction was expressed above all in the various forms of *negative theology*, according to which God could not be localised in time or space. At the same time, however, Christian faith is conscious that the God who transcends all our thinking and feeling *has made himself known in a definitive and unsurpassable way in Jesus Christ*, who was a concrete historical person. It is possible for us to learn from his appearance, his actions and his suffering, death and resurrection who God is and what his intentions are for man and human history. Following Jesus means that we must change our way of life and take our fellow-men and the world very seriously.

Neither our confession of Jesus as God-with-us nor our readiness to walk in his footsteps originate, however, in a personal encounter with the man Jesus. We only know him from a *tradition* in which he is expressed. He is mediated to us from a linguistic tradition and an extended world of images. *Popular religion is one of the ways in which this world of symbols is transmitted* and it constitutes the expression of our consent to the reality to which that language and those symbols point. Both the case for popular religiosity and the relative value of its legitimacy originate on the one hand in the tension that is always present in language, symbols and modes of expression and, on the other, in the reality to which those factors refer.

Translated by David Smith

Notes

1. Quoted by J. Duquesne 'Un Débat actuel: La religion populaire' *Religion populaire et Réforme liturgique* (Paris 1975) 10.
2. L. Maldonado *Genesis de catolicismo popular. El inconsciente colective de un proceso historico* (Madrid 1979) pp. 11–12.
3. See A. Vergote 'Volkskatholicisme' *Collationes* 9 (1979) 417–432.
4. See B. Hein 'Antonio Gramsci und die Volksreligion' in *Volksreligion—Religion des Volkes* ed. K. Rahner et al (Stuttgart 1979) pp. 156–164.
5. See A. Brants 'Volksreligiositeit en christelijk geloof' in *Volksreligiositeit: uitnodiging en uitdaging* ed. A. Blijlevens et al. (Averbode 1982) pp. 41–59.
6. See B. Welte *Die Würde des Menschen und die Religion. Anfrage an die Kirche in unserer Gesellschaft* (Frankfurt 1977).
7. See R. Towler *Homo Religiosus. Sociological Problems in the Study of Religion* (New York 1974).
8. See A. Vergote 'Dialogue interdisciplinaire sur l'Anthropologie sacramentelle' *MD* 119 (1974) 57.

9. The Venerable Bede *Historia Ecclesiastica Gentis Anglorum* 1.27.
10. See R. Schreiter *Constructing Local Theologies* (New York 1985) p. 130.
11. A. Brants, the article cited in note 5, at p. 54.
12. See H. Biezais 'Von der Wesensidentität der Religion und Magie' *A A Abo* A 557 (Abo 1978).
13. See R. Schreiter, the work cited in note 10, at pp. 137–138.

Enrique Dussel

Popular Religion as Oppression and Liberation: Hypotheses on its Past and Present in Latin America

THIS ESSAY is divided into five parts. First, I will discuss a particular theoretical approach to what *'popular* religion' is in Latin America. Second, I will investigate the historical development of the phenomenon. Third, I will offer a structural description of popular religion. Fourth, I will describe, in very general terms, the elements of this form of religion. Finally I will consider what is perhaps the most characteristic aspect of this religion, the whole area of its political significance, both from the point of view of its political manipulation and from that of its genuine potential for liberation.

1. INTRODUCTORY REMARKS

The Cuban Academy of Sciences recently established a department of sociology of religion. Last year I had discussions with its members on the theme 'Popular Religion in Cuba'. The subject is thus of interest in the most diverse areas of Latin American life.

(a) Popular culture

The phenomenon of 'popular religion' must be seen in the context of 'popular culture' in Latin America. By 'culture' I do not mean a level of the superstructure or an ideological level which is merely a 'reflection' of the infrastructure. Quite the contrary, 'culture' denotes a system of practical acts (beginning with those connected with production, the economy, etc.) which determine individual or social subjectivity, through labour and its products, through the relations of production themselves and through the existential meaning they have for subjectivity.

Culture is the totality of objects (material culture), with the world as a totality of meaning (intellectual culture) of which subjects (individuals, groups, classes, sectors of society, etc.) are the bearers. There is therefore a diversity of cultures, confrontation between them and domination of one culture over another. Cultures differ in extent; they may cover a class, a nation, a group of nations such as Latin America or a period of world history.

'Popular culture' is a specific culture,[1] and the popular culture of Latin America has its own quite specific stamp. If the 'people' is not the nation as a whole (this is the populist definition, which includes national bourgeoisies, as in Nazism, Fascism, Peronism, *cardenismo*, etc.), but the 'social bloc' of the oppressed, this means that the people includes the oppressed classes of the capitalist system (peasants and waged workers), and in addition tribes, ethnic groups, unemployed marginal groups and other oppressed social sectors, particularly in the outlying, dependent and under-developed nations of the capitalist world system. *Popular* culture is thus different from transnational or imperial culture, from the national culture, from the culture of the ruling classes, and even from 'mass' culture.[3]

(b) Popular religion in Latin America

The people's 'religion', especially in Latin America, is an element of popular culture. It is the *fundamental core of meaning* of popular culture as a whole, since in it practices are performed which define the deepest meaning of existence. The daily life of the suffering people of Latin America draws the meaning of life, work, marriage, the family, suffering and death, not from the State education system, not from the culture of the mass media, and not even from particular left-wing parties. It is the prerogative of popular religion to give meaning to all these areas.

At the same time this religion constitutes a core area of the people which is not distorted or counterfeit. It does so, on the one hand, because the nineteenth century liberal State was anti-popular, totally ignored the people and so enabled them to become the protagonists of their own religion. This is also true in the religious sphere, because the 'Romanisation' of Catholic Church in the second half of the nineteenth century distanced the Church too, in its official practices, from those practices in which the people themselves were the active subject. In other words, popular relgion remained under the control of the people themselves: in the family, in the village, in the neighbour-hood, in the lay confraternities, among the *rezadores*, community leaders, *mayordomos*, or simply in the faith of the people, over which official religion had no control, since it knew nothing of it.

This relation to actions, that is, the fact that people are in control of their activity and understand its structure, is what makes popular religion a privileged 'field' in which the people can assert their own interests, even if this process frequently remains merely symbolic.

In conclusion, then, we can say that popular religion consists of subjective popular beliefs, symbols and rites, of forms of behaviour and practices which have objective meaning, which are the product of a centuries-old history and should not be confused with the official clerical religion. It is a 'religious field' on its own, with relative autonomy, in which the people are the subject, even though priests, shamans and prophets also exercise influence.

2. HISTORICAL ORIGIN

Popular religion in Latin America is the result of a centuries-old historical process which has at least three main components.

(a) The beginning

(i) Hispanic and Lusitanian popular religion[4]

With the accession of Constantine the Roman empire became Christen-dom, and in the process Christianity became identified with the dominant culture. In addition, the Latin liturgy of Rome (one among many others) was despotically imposed on the mass of Christians. The combination of the establishment of the Roman liturgy as official and the development of the Christian community into a mass phenomenon, inevitably gave rise to feudal popular religion at the heart of medieval Christianity. This process occurred in the Roman imperial province of Hispania, which was ruled by the West Goths and was converted to Christianity in the sixth century. Hispanic 'popular religion' consisted of a whole bundle of tenets and practices, a mixture of the religious traditions of the Iberians and the Romans, those of the early Christians and the West Goths. As a result of the Moslem invasions it reached a new flowering in the Christian Arab structure. The apostle James cannot be understood unless he is seen as an anti-Mohammed in the reconquest of Spain from the Moors. Many popular religious traditions in

Latin America go back to Hispanic and Lusitanian, medieval and West Gothic origins.

(ii) Indian religion[5]

To a greater or lesser extent, according to the degree of contemporary presence of Indian culture, such as existed in Mexico and Central America, Peru, Ecuador and Bolivia, Latin American popular religion also derives from the traditions of the original inhabitants of the continent. Just as the Christianity of the Mediterranean region was superimposed on Greco-Roman religion (for example, Christmas derives from a pagan festival), and German Christianity on the religion of the original inhabitants (their trees and strikingly shaped rocks led to the development of symbolic religious elements, medieval places of pilgrimage and procession, out of pre-Christian altars and shrines), so the ancient beliefs and practices of the Caribbean Indians, the Aztecs, the Mayas, Chibchas or Incas, to mention only a few, are the soil on which Latin American religion has grown.

(iii) African religion

Because of their importance in the Caribbean, Central America, Brazil and Colombia, African religions must also be included among the constitutive elements of Latin American popular religion. The *orishas* express themselves in dances, and populate the everyday life of the Afro-American population of Latin America.

(b) The religion of Christendom in Latin America[6]

The violent clash at the conquest makes the presence of Christianity in Latin America deeply ambiguous. Nonetheless the quiet and often heroic work of thousands of Franciscans, Dominicans, Jesuits, Mercedarians and others resulted in an original and creative acceptance of the Gospel by the oppressed Indian people, mestizos, black slaves and impoverished Spaniards. This *people* developed, for itself, often in opposition to the dominant culture and even to the official Church, a *world* of religion, a system of beliefs and practices which gave meaning to the totality of daily life, work, struggles, pain, death, life after death, and so on. It was a Christian, but at the same time a Latin American, world. It was a world of its own, often unknown to the dominant classes, the dominant culture and religion and even those interested in it, a world which the intellectuals and the left-wing parties until recently despised, which the liberals ignored and the conservatives manipulated. This product of many centuries of popular life is today a fruitful field in which the old world which is passing away and the new one which is struggling to assert itself are locked in a life-and-death struggle.

(c) The period of development (nineteenth and twentieth centuries)

With the process of emancipation from Spain and Portugal popular religion became detached from the institutional Church and was transformed into an area of popular resistance to liberal rule, which was not only hostile to the conservatives, but also hostile to the people.

3. ESSENTIAL STRUCTURE

There is a form of populism which tends to turn everything to do with the people into a fetish without seeing that, as a result of the alienated oppression under which it lives, the people have incorporated their enemy and tyrant into their own religious structures. The people themselves transmit their own oppression from generation to generation in their tradition. Because of this, sharp and fundamental distinctions must be made.

(a) Popular religion as oppression

To analyse the negative, alienating aspects the following structure is helpful. It is based on the description given by Gilberto Gimenez, using the categories of linguistics,[7] specifically the 'actors' model of Propp or Greimas.[8]

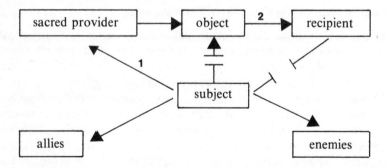

Since the Christian people (the subject), in its state of oppression, poverty and exploitation, cannot attain to the goods necessary for everyday life (the object), health, food, work, housing, education, good harvests, safe travel, etc., it transfers responsibility for these goods to the Lord, the saint, the deity (the sacred provider), who bestows the desired object through miracles or special gifts. In this way the subject is active in worship (arrow 1), but a passive recipient of the gifts (arrow 2).

In this way the daily life of the dominated and oppressed people takes place in an 'other world' beyond the secular everyday. In reality everything is holy. Every action is governed by rules: the way of eating, the way of greeting, prayers, domestic worship, the sanctuaries of the saints, lighting candles. One has to win the sympathy of the 'allies' (the saints, the 'souls in purgatory', etc.); and one must defend oneself against the enemies (the devil, curses, etc.). The religious dimension permeates the whole of life; the 'actors' are numerous and demanding. In the country, in the villages, in the poor quarters of the towns, everywhere people live in a sort of 'mythical space'. Life suffocates in transcendence. It is a perfectly controlled system.

Belief in the survival of the soul after death, for example, is a central element in popular religion. All the fears of rural people feed on this. Apparitions, ghosts, the cries and rustling of souls in the night make it necessary to practice soothsaying, displaying a knife handle as a cross and crossing oneself with growing devotion. Popular theology, with its angels and devils, with its spirits of nature and the other world, with its souls in purgatory, forms the main substance of our legends and myths.[9]

(b) Popular religion as liberation

However, the field of popular religion is not totally in the hands of shamans; it also has room for prophets. It is a field of conflict, and for that reason can serve the interests of the dominated classes, in other words, liberation.[10]

In this case the function of the 'actors' changes. The protagonists become historical. The 'sacred provider' is the people itself (arrow 1), which produces

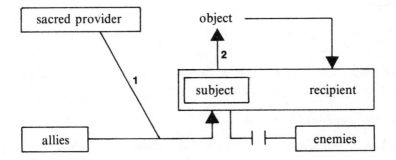

heroes and saints from its midst and attains its object practically (arrow 2). The gift or miracle consists in the fact that the people themselves become the protagonists of history.

A good example to demonstrate the change of model is the process of Mexican emancipation; another, which we will describe towards the end of this article, is Nicaragua today.

When the Aztecs invaded the upper valley of Mexico, they subdued the peasant population of the country. 'The highest of their goddesses was called Cihuacóatl, that is, "snake woman", whom they called Tonantzin,' stated Sahagun in his *General History of New Spain.*[11] The famous temple of 'Tonantzin-tla' ('our little mother') still exists today. Thus the aggressive warrior Huitzilopochtli, the (Aztec) god of the sky, subdued the cultivators (worshippers of the female goddess of fertility). At a sanctuary of Tonantzin in Tepeyac, to which the oppressed at the time of the Aztecs came in pilgrimage, the image of our Lady of Guadalupe was later honoured, the Virgin associated with the reconquest of Spain from the Moors. The oppressed class, the indigenous peoples, and later the creoles (since Miguel Sanchez's work of 1648 on *The image of the Virgin Mary, the Mother of God of Guadalupe, which miraculously appeared in Mexico*[12]) found in this Virgin, the object of popular devotion, first support for the creation of a national Mexican and anti-Spanish consciousness and later the flag of the emancipation struggles. In 1800 a group of patriots called themselves the 'Guadalupes'. The priest Hidalgo used the flag and the colours of the Virgin of Gudalupe for his army, as did Morelos, while the Spaniards grouped themselves under the banner of the Virgin of Perpetual Succour, which Cortes had saved from the Aztecs in the 'sad night'. In the twentieth century Zapata took Cuernavaca under the banner of the Virgin of Guadalupe, and César Chavez, the leader of the Californian farmworkers' union, is making the Virgin of Guadalupe the driving force of his movement today. In this way a popular religious symbol has become a force for change and the basis of liberation.

4. THE MAIN CONTENTS

Latin American popular religion contains particular practices, whose contents can be described schematically as follows.

(a) The sacralisation of time

'Time' is essentially a religious boundary; neither the economic time of two-weekly or monthly payments nor contracts of employment are measured by *fiestas*. The first short period of time to be sacralised is the day, as a person crosses themselves on leaving the house for work and before eating and sleeping, and similarly in other religious practices during the day.

In a medium period such as a year the thread of religion runs through the whole course of the seasons (particularly in the country, but no less so in the city). Winter is the season of death, spring the season of resurrection of life. The feasts of patron saints derive in practice from ancient totem cults and a long tradition. Important moments are Holy Week, earlier carnival, All Saints and the festivals of the dead.

There is a still longer period, that of a people's history. The people guards the memory of its heroes, its saints and its heroic deeds, which are of supreme importance, particularly in moments of liberation.

(b) The sacralisation of space

Similarly the people enjoys a degree of 'centrality' (the family, the village, the neighbourhood, the district). Everything else is 'peripheral'. The road from one space into the other is something to be negotiated, that from home to factory or to another village (travel is dangerous), and so people must entrust themselves to a saint, an ally or a similar figure. Processions, and above all pilgrimages are a 'road' through profane space towards the centrality of the consecrated space *par excellence*, the shrine of the Virgin of Guadalupe, those of Copacabana, the Christ of 'Gran Poder' or Esquipula. As long as the religious practice lasts, for a short time there is some control over the space of 'transition', which may be hostile but is now controlled by the people. The people occupies and controls space by its number, and so simultaneously achieves self-affirmation.

(c) The sacralisation of rhythm

A basic expression of popular religion is rhythm, movements to the beat of music, the 'drumbeat' dances to the rhythm of the rumba rattles, the harp, the guitar, the marimba or the *charras*, which in Bolivia are made of bull horns. The rhythm of the year, the month, week or the day is speeded up in the rhythm of the sacred dance, in which the body is united with the rite, in the rhythm of prayer and even ecstasy; this takes place to a much greater degree in the *umbanda* or *candomblé*, in voodoo or other Afro-American forms.

(d) The objects of worship

Popular religion addresses itself in a spirit of faith to the following persons, powers and spirits as objects. The 'God of the poor' is the *Eternal Father*, who is ever-present and to whom the people normally turn, and who expresses himself in specific actions: in rain, in good harvests, health and safe journeys. He is just and kindly; he is faithful, but also often the cause of evil and misfortune, before which the only possible attitude is resignation. It is well-known that the *blessed Virgin* has replaced the goddesses of cultivators and peasants, who were mother goddesses, and ever since has occupied a central place in Latin America. She is closer than the Eternal Father; she is the compassionate mother. Among Blacks, former slaves, she is Yemandá, the mother of water. Rather than as a historical figure, *Jesus Christ* is depicted in the garb of many 'Christs': there are 'Christs' and 'Lords' with many names and in many places. He is even shown as the *niño*, a child; for example, the leader of the locality or community is called *Niño Alcalde*. The same is true of the *cross*; it is less the historical instrument of his death, but a force against the devil. It hangs by roadsides, on mountains, on the walls of proletarian houses, and they are erected on the roof ridges of houses by the builders: 'For the sake of the holy cross, Lord, free us from all evil'.[13] Particularly striking are the *images of the crucified Jesus,* baroque images of Christ drenched in pain and blood, which depict the sacrifice of the exploited people themselves.

And finally the *saints*: the patrons of the family, districts, villages, communities, of every place. Many of these have been superimposed on ancient divinities, natural forces or principles. There is a saint for everything, to ensure that a girl finds a husband, for faithfulness, fertility, to find lost objects, etc. The dead, and good and bad 'spirits', are also among the objects of worship. Death, with whom a person will hold a relaxed conversation, who is even called 'St Death', is a normal partner in conversations among the people.

Nor, among the Afro-American population, can the 'spirits' (*orishás*) be ignored. They are the object of a special cult and overlap with the saints. What dancers express in ecstasy is a supremely religious world.

Overall we encounter a world populated by protagonists. To the outsider, the person who does not enter this world, it seems ordinary, boring or tragic. For the participants it offers a multiplicity of practices rich in meaning.

(e) The ethos of popular religion

In general the normal 'attitude' to history, to personal and social life, is tragic and passive. Everything is coloured by a certain theology of resignation: 'It's the will of God,' where 'it' may be the death of a child, illness, loss of a job or death. At least everything has a meaning in popular religion but, as we have noted, sometimes it is a reflection of the dominant ideology in the dominated themselves.

5. CURRENT POLITICAL MEANING

In contrast to what has taken place in the central developed countries, the process of secularisation which derived from the Enlightenment never really penetrated to the oppressed people in the Third World (Africa, Asia and Latin America). As a result of poverty, suffering and exploitation the people were never able to share the wealth or the values of capitalism. Secularisation was possible only in a capitalism which no longer needed any religious justification of its rule: surplus value was extracted without the awareness of either property-owner or worker. There was therefore no need to justify it, since no-one regarded it as injustice. Since the people of the peripheral countries could never enjoy the achievements of capitalism, they preserved their traditions. And it does not look as though these traditions will disappear in the future.

(a) Populist manipulation

Popular religion in Latin America is 'manipulated' on at least three levels. First there are the shamans or 'deceivers' (the old priests in modernised form) who 'operate' with soothsaying, healing through prayer, herbs and blessings. They should be distinguished from traditional medicine. Shamanism is the decadent form of the tradition.

Secondly, political society itself and the populist State (such as those of Perón, Vargas, Rojas Pinilla, etc.) 'use' popular religion to control the people (as did Duvalier until recently). In contrast to the nineteenth-century liberals, who despised Christianity because of its bourgeois, dependent ideology, the populist leaders made links with the people with a gloss of religious charisma (perhaps with the exception of Cárdenas in Mexico).

Thirdly, the official Catholic Church also 'used' popular religion. As mentioned above, the 'Romanisation' of the Catholic Church since the second half of the nineteenth century divided it from popular religion. In reality two sorts of religious practices exist side by side, on the one side those of the people and on the other the official ones. The people, the *mayordomo* or the lay confraternities escort the saint in procession so that the 'father' (the official priest) can, for example, say a mass for him or her. But the two sets of practices have different meanings. In fact they are two different religions. Nonetheless the hierarchical Catholic Church continues to control the centres of pilgrimage and the shrines, and it is clearly aware of this coexistence—i.e., it manipulates.

(b) The liberating character of popular religion

Different attitudes to Latin American popular religion are, however, possible, attitudes which do not consist in populist manipulation but continue the process which has begun and carry it to a conclusion.

The first feature which deserves mention is the widespread experience of the so-called 'basic ecclesial communities'. They are firmly rooted in the people; they are the people. They are a new creation from within popular religion. The members of basic communities are adherents of popular religion. By reappropriating God's word (the Bible), they can see their earlier experience in a historical context, relate it to the present and politicise it. They relate them to the present on a new level of consciousness. Without ceasing to be traditional popular religion, this level now acquires a prophetic, critical, creative and political significance. The members deny nothing in their old beliefs, devotions and practices, but they now understand them in a different context, in a new framework of conscious faith, responsible action, organisation, political demands and political action as service. They do this in the name of the same patrons, the same Virgin of Luján, the *Aparecida*, the same Christ of 'Gran Poder' or of Esquipula. This is a religion which begins to move in history.

Secondly, popular religion can, in certain cases, become motivation for acts of liberation and changes, and release a heroic and collective enthusiasm, just as they previously kept the oppressed trapped in the ideology of the oppressor. Just as, since 1808, the Virgin of Guadalupe has stimulated the action of men like Miguel Hidalgo, Morelos or Pavon, so today, for example in Nicaragua, it is not just Christian élites which have taken part in liberation movements. In Nicaragua, alongside the group known as the 'Proletarians', one of the three which founded the Sandinista Front, which consisted of Christians such as *Comandante* Luis Carrion, *Comandante* Wheelock, *Comandante* Mónica Valtodano, etc. the people themselves, the basic communities, ordinary Christian families took up the struggle against Somoza and his oppressive regime because of their faith. It was this which led the FSLN itself to declare on 8 October 1980 in an official document 'On Religion':

Some writers have said that religion is a tool for the alienation of people and serves to justify the exploitation of one class by another. This statement, no doubt, has historical value to the degree that in other historical periods religion offered theoretical support for political domination.
But the FSLN continues:

However, we Sandinistas affirm that our experience shows that when Christians, motivated by their faith, are capable of responding to the needs of the people and history, their beliefs drive them to revolutionary activity. Our experience has shown that it is possible to be a believer and a committed revolutionary at the same time and that there is no irreconcilable contradiction between the two.

The FSLN could make this statement because of the practices of a Christian people which had confirmed its Christian identity in the war of liberation. The mother made the sign of the cross in front of her dead son, took his body and brought it into the church, where a liturgy was celebrated for him as for a hero. Before the battle the young soldiers knelt, made the sign of the cross, asked the Mary Immaculate for help ... and began to fight. In the north of Esteli I have heard peasants explaining, Bible in hand: 'We are like Nehemiah and Ezra. With one hand we are building the walls of Jerusalem' (they were defending with arms the northern border of Nicaragua against the 'contras' paid by Reagan), 'and with the other we are building the temple, our basic ecclesial community.'

Popular religion is centuries-old and modern, it is faithful and revolutionary, like the indigenous peoples who rebelled in the colonial period (like Tupac Amaru, who saw himself as Moses fighting against Pharaoh), and like the national heroes of the nineteenth century. This is the religion of the Nicaraguan people who met Pope John Paul II with a giant poster showing a picture of the people and beside them St Dominic (the Dominicans were the first missionaries) and our Lady of the Immaculate Conception (the Nicaraguan national religious symbol), all under a slogan which would have been unintelligible on another continent, in Europe—in Poland perhaps: 'Welcome, John Paul II. Thank God and the revolution.'

Only Latin American popular religion can create such a synthesis. It emerged among the indigenous people defeated by the Spaniards and Portuguese. It flowered among slaves and the oppressed. It is alive in the areas on the edges of cities, in impoverished rural areas and in the destitution of an exploited people, dominated and oppressed. But, trusting in God, believing in his providence, that people waits like the 'Christ of patience' (seated, with the crown of thorns, head in hand, his elbow supported on his knee) for crucifixion—but also for liberation.

Translated from the author's German by Francis McDonagh

Notes

1. See my article 'Cultura latinoamericana y Filosofia de la liberacion' *Cristianismo y Sociedad* 80 (1984) 9–45. See further E. Dussel *Historia General de la Iglesia en América Latina* I/I (Salamanca 1983); *idem, Historia de la Iglesia en América Latina—Coloniaje y liberación 1492–1983* (Mexico 1983); *El Catolicismo popular en la Argentina* (History) (Buenos Aires 1969) (bibliography pp 167–233); CEHILA 'Religiosidade popular na América Latina' *Revista de Cultura Vozes* 4 (1979); Seladoc team *Religiosidad Popular* (Salamanca 1976); R. Azzi *O episcopado do Brasil frente*

ao catolocismo popular (Petrópolis 1977); E. Bosi *Cultura de massa e cultura popular—leituras de operárias* (Petrópolis 3° 1977); Various *Fe cristiana y revolución sandinista en Nicaragua* (Managua 1980); G. Giménez *Cultura popular y religión en el Anáhuac* (Mexico 1978); CELAM *Iglesia y religiosidad popular en América Latina* (Bogota 1977); E. Hoornaert *Formação do catolicismo brasileiro 1550-1800* (Petrópolis 2° 1978); G.P. Süss *Volkskatholizismus in Brasilken* (Munich and Mainz 1978); *Religiosidad y fe en América Latina* ed. M. Jorda (Santiago 1975); *idem. La sabiduriá de un pueblo* (Santiago 1975); *idem. El catolicismo criollo*, (Santiago 1975); CELAM *Los grupos afroamericanos—Aproximaciones y pastoral* (Bogota 1980).

    2. See E. Dussel *Para leer los Grundrisse* Chap. 18.

    3. See E. Dussel 'Cultura Latinoamericana' the article cited in note 1.

    4. See E. Dussel *Historia General*, the work cited in note 1, at pp 157ff; 196ff; 566ff.

    5. See *ibid.* pp 103ff (the religious prehistory of Latin America).

    6. See *idem.* pp 281ff (the evangelisation of Latin America); *ibid.* 561ff (everyday life).

    7. See *ibid.*

    8. A.J. Greimas *Sémantique structurale* (Paris 1966); V. Propp *Morphologie du conte* (Paris 1970).

    9. O. di Lullo *El espírito cristiano en el folklore de Santiago* (Tucuman 1943) p. 352.

    10. See O. Maduro *Religión y conflicto social* (Mexico 1981).

    11. Book I, Chap. 6 (III, Mexico 1956)p. 352.

    12. Imprenta Calderón (Mexico 1648).

    13. E. Zeballos *Cancionero popular* (Buenos Aires 1891) p. 68.

Part III

Popular Religion as a Challenge to Church Practice

Giuseppe Ruggieri

Popular Faith, Ecclesiastical Strategy and Religious Needs

AT LEAST since the time of Gregory the Great, pastors and theologians, faced with the phenomenon of popular religion, have formulated a *tactic of absorption* that can in very general terms be said to be based on two convictions: that the people are incapable of following the Gospel in its purity; and that religious beliefs and practices foreign to the Gospel can be taken over, since then they are clearly integrated into the Christian religion and purified of pagan motives.[1]

To what extent have 'the people' gone along with these tactics? Those who try to give a historical answer to this question, to the extent that it has an accessible history, are well aware of the difficulties in this approach: historians, in fact, argue to this day over the effective degree of 'Christianisation' of Europe right down to modern times. I propose to limit my remarks here to the question in Italy in the post-Tridentine period, but even within these limits, pastoral strategy has oscillated between a rigorous approach refusing to admit any concession to religious practices that did not conform to the purity of the early Church (an approach shown in moderation by Antonio Muratori and in more extreme form by the Italian Jansenists of the latter part of the eighteenth century), and a more 'possibilist' approach, practiced by the Jesuits and many bishops in the South, though to varying degrees.

In more recent times there have been *two main approaches to popular religion* (though these two are not mutually exclusive and more nuanced than

97

this summary presentation might suggest). The first, stemming from Antonio Gramsci (one of the founders of the Italian Communist party, who realised the inadequacy of the classic Marxist interpretation), sees popular religion as the channel through which the traditionally deprived sectors of society express their nostalgia for a different human condition, but also their particular riches, their special zest for life and their culture. This interpretation tends to see religious feeling and popular religion as an alternative to the official religion of the Church. The other approach rejects this alternative: popular religion has no class significance and is not confined to the 'lower' classes. 'Religious practice, even when interwoven in a framework of magic and superstition, is found in all classes: manual labourers, peasants, tenant farmers, large landowners, and even the clergy.'[2]

I propose to develop these brief reflections on different lines from those sketched out above. Beyond the valuable contributions made by the disciplines of history and anthropology, there is the pastoral interest of those who wish to spread the hope and promise of the Christian Gospel among the mass of the people. This pastoral interest tends to see the situation not in static terms, used for the sake of a neat interpretation, but in its possibilities, contradictions and openness, allowing itself to be guided by one precise question: How does one believe, be converted, experience Christian life now, in the particular cultural situation in which it is one's lot to live? With this interest as guide, I should like to develop some thoughts that will necessarily be both limited and problematical.

The *limits* are set by the extent of my experience: certain typical situations in *Southern Italy and above all in Sicily*. The problematic, however, springs from a clear conviction, non-problematic in itself, that popular religion is just one of the signs pointing to the *need for the Church radically to change its own stance with regard to society*. There are still, at least, as far as I know, few studies carried out from this viewpoint.[3] The usual approaches are made either from an anthropological standpoint or from that of a certain ecclesiastical astuteness.[4] This astuteness is characterised by a willingness to adapt, but an effective lack of openness to being questioned. The problem of popular religion here seems to be firstly a matter of conversion from a sort of conqueror's mentality.

1. WHERE CONFRONTATION TAKES PLACE

The first consideration is where confrontation between popular religion and the official Church might be said to take place. The researches of cultural anthropology over the past decade have emphasised the value of popular devotions and festivals least tied to the official liturgy of the Church. It is certainly not my intention to play down the importance of these manifestations for understanding the spirit and culture of the people. Yet in the present pastoral situation it seems false to give them too much importance as a way of understanding the dialectic existing between the 'official' mentality of the Church and that of the people. I should like to make a few observations about festivals and popular devotional manifestations that seem to me to reduce their importance in relation to the question under discussion.

(a) Even in the South of Italy, such religious manifestations always fall short of involving *all the people*. The younger generations do not fully grasp their significance and increasingly regard them as foreign to their interests. Today the mass media increasingly iron out cultural differences and modify the language. The 'regional' language of such manifestations has therefore become accessible only to the older generations.

(b) After a phase of criticism and 'purification' of such manifestations, there is now a more generalised sort of 'peaceful co-existence' between the clergy and the people. This co-existence has the effect of making the meanings seen in them by the people (the saint still seen as a numinous and tremendous power, the tragic symbolisation of existence, etc.) have their expressive value, but remain basically inoperative. Religious imagination, culturally in decline, does not use these events to produce meanings that have any innovatory significance in everyday life.

(c) The deepest manifestations of popular religiosity in southern Italy are linked to the *rites of Holy Week* and therefore are of a piece with the official liturgy of the Church, at least as the people see it.

(d) Besides the rites of Holy Week, the usual and proper celebration of the sacraments should be borne in mind. The people of the South do not regard baptism, marriage and funerals as 'foreign', less 'theirs' than popular devotions. In fact, these sacramental occasions, in the context of the progressive waning of old devotional manifestations, but also independently of this waning, form the chief context in which the religious sense of existence is expressed. This statement holds good for the past too, as an historical example will indicate. In his *'ad limina'* report, a seventeenth-century bishop of Catania in Sicily, Mgr. Branciforte, relates how the poor were often subjected to really harsh demands for money by the priests celebrating the sacraments, to the extent that when the priest refused to administer the sacraments, particularly baptism and funeral rites, without receiving his due 'fee', those who had no money were obliged to seek loans at exorbitant rates of interest, often from the priest himself.[5] The people's attachment to the sacraments cannot be explained by the simple obligation on them to receive them; besides the ecclesiastical and social 'constraint' to do so, there is the deeper conviction of a Christian dimension of the dignity of existence. This conviction is felt apart from the mediation of the Church, and often in conflict with it. Even today one can see that clerical mediation, and institutional interference in general, is 'put up with' rather than accepted. Such a statement would need to be documented and verified from a variety of geographical situations, but here it will have to be enough to have noted the fact.

In any case, a first conclusion should be clear: where confrontation between the official Church and popular religion takes place is now *not outside the official liturgy of the Church itself*. This, in my view, is the central focus of the confrontation, and it is just this fact that gives rise to far-reaching problems.

2. POPULAR RELIGION OR POPULAR FAITH?

A second consideration is the very nature of popular religion in southern Italy. In my view the term popular 'religion' is inadequate if we are to tackle the problem from a theological and pastoral standpoint. Even if anthropologists are justified in using the language of comparative religion, the limits imposed by this language make it inadequate for discussing the question in terms of Christian practice. For example, the religious expression of the people of Sicily is deeply marked by the historical memory of Christianity. At the centre of this expression is the *image of the suffering Christ*, and even more so of the *dead* Christ. Sicilian religious imagination has built its most consistent symbolisations around the figure of Christ taken down from the cross and accompanied to the tomb by his sorrowing mother (I am consciously using the title 'Christ', although the Sicilian people would use 'Jesus' to describe the one who is taken down from the cross and taken to the tomb). These symbolisations come to express the central contents of their religious feeling: the Christian dignity of man's death and of every woman's suffering. In other words, death and suffering have their own, non-instrumental dignity, which can only be contemplated and which is accompanied *in silence*.

In my view, we must here speak, even if with caution, of a genuine form of Christian *faith*. It is a matter of *concentrating* faith itself in just some aspects of the historical memory of Christianity, in which the theme of death has become almost obsessive. One almost forgotten practice is significant here: their celebration of the Paschal vigil, particularly before the last reform which made it a night-time celebration, which was observed by the people in some parts of Sicily not in the churches, but in the cemeteries. They waited by the tombs of their dead relatives for the ringing of the Easter bells, which came as a proclamation of hope.

The nucleus of this popular faith can therefore be described as a sort of identification between the historical suffering and death of Christ and the present experience of human suffering and death. Human experience takes on dignity and meaning in this identification. That is, it becomes possible to live this concrete existence without being overwhelmed by it, to keep it open to a future which cannot be seen, but which is not denied either.

One sometimes gets the impression that other aspects of existence, such as joy and success, remain on this side of the encounter between Christianity and experience, almost at a still pagan, basically dionysiac, stage. Not that moments of joyous representation are absent from religious festivals, but they give the impression that they have not yet been integrated, not been marked with Christian memory, but simply 'housed' in the ritual celebration.

This popular faith is therefore summed up in a confused sense of the depth of human existence, particularly where the abyss of nothingness yawns. In this confused sense of the depth and dignity of existence it is sometimes difficult to separate openness to mystery from acceptance of fate, hope from consciousness of historical defeat. The memory of human suffering is inextricably linked to the memory of Christ's passion, focussed in a silence—a silence that becomes as overpowering as the mountains during the Good Friday processions—and a waiting whose outcome is uncertain and in suspense. This is therefore not an example of pure and purified faith, but of a concrete historical image of human longing and recall, open to various possibilities.

This is the faith that the Church, in its daily pastoral practice, has to deal with. It is in the name of this faith that virtually all the people of southern Italy still ask for baptism, and, to a lesser but consistent extent, for Christian celebration of their weddings and funerals.

3. A MUTE CATECHESIS

Their requests for these celebrations do not therefore spring from a response to the teaching of the Church, but as a *felt need to confirm and root their own historical recall.* And this is where confrontation arises between popular faith, the historical representation of religious need, and the official pastoral practice of the Church. The everyday practice of many parishes is today extensively bound up in dealing with this confrontation.

Over the last several decades, but especially since Vatican II, the Church has sought to play a *more active role.* It is no longer content, as it was in the past, to react to the demands and act on them, but now lays down a *course of catechesis* which must precede reception of any sacrament.

The *contents of this catechesis*, except for any variants that may be introduced as a result of the human and spiritual sensitivity of those who give the course, show ignorance, if one may say so, of the real motives behind a request for baptism. Its contents are rather determined by the requirement to clarify the theological meaning of the sacrament—conversion, insertion in the community, union with Christ, etc.

I do not think it is an exaggeration to say that *only a minority of the people* (mostly from the less 'popular' classes) *accept and understand this catechesis.* For most of them it is rather a strange condition that, for some years in these parts, the clergy have imposed on those Christians who wish to have their children baptised.

The most conscientious pastoral workers therefore find themselves in something of a *dilemma.* On one hand they recognise both the authenticity and the ambiguity of a historical memory that they do not feel able either to reject or to accept outright. On the other, they too are prisoners of the abstractness of the official catechesis, which is couched in a language that cannot be put across, because it is mute and strange in relation to everyday speech. It cannot be put across not because it derives from the language of the cross, hard though this is for sinful man; it cannot be put across because it is a strange jargon, formulated according to the requirements of theological continuity, but detached from the experience of suffering and therefore mute, however full of sound.

What emerges is therefore a *sort of compromise.* While a minority of the faithful succeed in understanding the prescribed catechesis, the majority just listen patiently. The pastoral worker, content with the attention he has received, therefore agrees to celebrate the sacrament.

This celebration then explodes as a 'religious' celebration for the family in all its deepest relationships, as a religious and social seal set on its doings and expectations. But it is a seal that the group sets on itself, even if it is 'housed' in a ritual celebration of the Church. This ritual celebration will be followed elsewhere by a more meaningful convivial celebration of the affections and bonds of the family group.

What has taken place here is not therefore an encounter between a historical subject, in the specificity of his and her memory, sufferings and joys on the one hand and, on the other, a believing community that feels this subject to be a brother and sister, a fellow citizen of the city of the saints, a participator in their same hopes. What has taken place is the ritual enactment of basic incommunicability between a Church trying to adapt and renew, within the confines of its own mental universe, its own actions and language, and a progressively derivative culture, increasingly prey to new emergent languages and ever more destined to lose its identity to stronger languages and cultures.

4. THE POSSIBLE FUTURE OF WHAT HAS NO FUTURE

Without claiming to have exhausted the question, I have tried to sketch some of the problems attendant on the confrontation between some forms of popular faith, as they still survive in parts of southern Italy, and the official pastoral practice of the Church. I should like finally to add a few rapid thoughts as a sort of provocative conclusion:

(a) The future of this particular form of popular religiosity is, in my view, tied to the *destiny of an increasingly peripheral culture*, ever more subjected to invasion by stronger cultures. The cultural empire of the West becomes daily more monolithic. The historical subjects under discussion are about to suffer the *n*th and most radical invasion of their entire history. Sicily has always been a place to invade, from the Phoenicians to the Greeks, from the Romans to the Byzantines, from the Arabs to the Normans, and so on down to our own times, when invasions continue in the shape of nuclear bases, planetary cultures, uniform languages.

(b) The problem, then, is how to assure a future for the substance of this popular faith, the wisdom accumulated through a history of defeats and sufferings great and small, age-old and everyday. I have tried to isolate the substance of this popular faith, historically linked to the Christian faith, as a particular experience of death and suffering, as the *inevitable mystery* of existence itself, not to be rationalised, not to be trivialised, not to be absorbed in any ideological system, but to be maintained intact in the collective memory.

(c) The churches can contribute to this historical task, which is also an essential aspect of their mission in the world, not by grinding the powder of abstract theological language ever finer, but in a presence composed of *Christian poverty and freedom*. What in fact often hinders effective understanding of the demands made by popular faith is just the screen erected by the historical weight of formulas and gestures, by a habit of divorcing the Church's life and culture from common experience.

· (d) If this poor and free presence in the midst of the brothers and sisters who remain dumb in the face of the drama of death and suffering is to be possible, it will not be enough for the Church to 'touch up' its own catechesis and liturgical celebrations. A Church that looks to its own salvation above all else will in fact be incapable of becoming this presence in the midst of the brethren and sisterhood. The Church is called first to acquire freedom, the ability to sit effectively at table with all sorts of women and men and to work in harmony with all those who knock at its door. Only when there is an effective participation in the daily drama of members of the community, a discreet taking on of their burdens, a common suffering and a common rejoicing with them, only then will it be possible for every individual historical person to be welcomed with respect.

(e) It is only within the context of 'a practice of holiness' (hardly touched on here) that it makes sense to work out a catechesis that, in the state of foreignness that Christianity finds itself in sociologically, is no longer just catechesis but always at the same time strong proclamation, evangelisation of the poor of the earth: that is, a proclamation that the Kingdom of God is at the gates, that our human adventure is always kept open to the presence of mystery, that hope can never be denied. And only within this practice of holiness will celebrations be possible that unite the Christian memory to the human memory of suffering, in which our ritual meals are 'truly the Lord's supper' as Paul says (1 Cor. 11:20) and no longer a hypocritical re-establishment of the distance that separates some of the sisters and brothers from others in the Church.

Translated by Paul Burns

Notes

1. The thought of Gregory the Great is summed up in his letter to the monk Mellitus, in which, among other things, he comments on the habit of sacrificing oxen practised by the English, that they no longer do this to the devil, but to the glory of God, giving thanks to the author of all things for having eaten their fill. Original Latin text in *Venerabilis Bedae hist. eccles. gentis anglorum*, ed. C. Plummer (Oxford 1896) I p. 63.

2. G. De Rosa *Chiesa e religione populare nel Mezzogiorno* (Bari 1979) p. VI.

3. For a first methodological study, see D. Pizzuti-Giannoni *Fede popolare* (Turin 1979); see also the summary by B.M. Bosatra 'Recenti miscellanee sulla religione popolar' in *La Scuola cattolica* 110 (1982) 65-84, 300-313.

4. For a general view and the results of research, see D. Pizzuti-Giannoni, the work cited in note 3; also the pertinent observations of C. Russo 'La religiosità popolare nell'età moderna. Problemi e prospettive' in *Problemi di storia della chiesa nei secoli XVII-XVIII* (Naples 1982) pp. 137-90.

5. See A. Longhitano 'Le relazioni "ad limina" della diocesi di Catania 1640-1646' in *Synaxis 2* (1984) 281-446.

Osmar Erwin Gogolok

Pastoral Aspects of Popular Religion in Brazil

1. POPULAR RELIGIOSITY

THE ELECTION of a *civilian President* after twenty years of a military regime was an occasion for the Brazilian people to rejoice at the beginning of 1985. When the elected Presidnt, Tancredo Neves, fell sick before his induction and was grappling with death, the Brazilian people were united in desire and prayer for his recovery. In this historic moment differences of religion and denomination were meaningless. All Brazil pleaded for the life of this *symbol of their aspirations.* Afro-Brazilian cultic shrines were erected in front of the hospital where Tancredo was fighting for his life. Special masses were said for him. Catholics were kneeling next to animists. Penitential crosses and rosaries, sacrifices for Oxala and invocations of destructive cosmic forces demonstrated so strong a religiousness that the officials of the various religions and denominations were astonished. When the President died they feared the results of disenchantment and hastened to offer their interpretations. The Rabbi of Sao Paulo said: 'Like Moses Tancredo was taken up to the mountain top to see the Promised Land'.[1] The Brazilian Bishops' Conference indicated that the human events had to be seen in the light of faith—which was what the people had been doing at their devotions for the past month—and said: 'This long and bitter vigil of the entire nation revealed and fixed the unity of Brazil in one belief, in a heart, and in convincing and confident faith in prayer for the sick man and for Brazil'.[2]

105

The anthropologist Ruben César Fernandes interpreted the spontaneous religious phenomenon thus: 'In this crisis a common prayer had a more inclusive significance. The individual—Tancredo—and the collective—Brazil—were united. People prayed simultaneously for Tancredo and for Brazil and thus took on themselves the mortal struggle of "being a Brazilian"'[3]

The sociologist Pedro de Oliveira showed that religion was not merely something for the country-people but was still meaningful for city-dwellers. The religiousness which had been suppressed into the private realm needed only a single event as catalyst to flourish again spontaneously.[4] The references of many uncertain commentators to magic and mysticism missed the real nature of this historic expression of popular religiosity. It was a case of common handling of a threatening event, of forces of survival, of resistance, and of the drawing of a common meaning from a given socio-religious identity.

2. 'RELIGION OF THE PEOPLE'

The *values of popular religiousness are recognised by the institutional Church in Latin America* and are seen as a task and challenge in the context of evangelisation (Puebla No. 444–469; *Evangelii nuntiandi* 48). A Brazilian author has made an attempt to analyze and interpret these texts.[5] An open and positive attitude to popular religion emerged from an opinion poll of pastoral office-holders in the North East of Brazil. There is an emphasis on replacing the often negatively nuanced term 'popular religiosity' by the term 'popular religion'. The question of the pastoral value of this religion is seen as outdated. Positive experiences and references to due consideration of the people of God are advanced in an integral pastoral policy as against a premature analysis of the situation. One of the most important aspects of the pastoral approach is in question here. There have certainly already been conflicts or tension between the clergy and the pastoral functionaries of popular piety. The deprecatory attitude more often met with earlier has largely given way to respect and a certain fascination. The more strongly the ecclesiastical elements of basic communities come to carry weight, the more one happens on popular religious characteristics.

The *'small communities'* or 'comunidades de inserção' of the Orders which have emerged from the option for the poor exist in the margin of existing official religious Order and Church structures; in the slums they encounter the religion of the people but find that it is more popular than their own religious forms, and discover anew the unity of faith and life. Investigations and extension seminars offer possibilities of making these impulses to a renewed pastoral effort effective in various ways.

As a pastoral service the Brazilian Bishops' Conference (CNBB) has published through its liturgical commission a *comprehensive bibliography on popular religiosity*. It refers to the impetus of Medellin and finds the intention of Puebla further strengthened. The 216 titles cited on Afro-Brazilian cults show that considerable preliminary scholarly work has been carried out in this regard. With 121 titles, the studies on animism or spiritism are also quite far-reaching. There is a very concise list of works on Indian religions. Popular medicine and music required their own chapter.[6] In 1984, on the occasion of the twentieth anniversary of the constitution on the sacred liturgy of Vatican II, a seminar on 'Popular Religiosity and Liturgy' was held at Fortaleza-Ceará under the aegis of the regional group Nordeste 1 of the CNBB. The bishops and other pastoral office-bearers have discovered that the Church is more effectively present in the expressions of popular religion than in many official liturgical acts. Unity of faith and life and popular witness demand a change of position. The *wisdom of the people* has been rediscovered. It has had an encouraging effect on existing pastoral officials. The bishops were discomfited at having to pass on from the Congregation for Sacred Rites to groups committed to the emancipation of the Black population a rejection of the 'Missa dos Quilombos' (Mass of the fortified slave villages) and the quasi-popular 'Missa da Terra sem Males' (Mass of the country without wrongdoing) on the ground that they exceeded liturgical norms.[7]

3. 'CAMINHADA'

If the biblical event of Exodus is seen as the norm of pastoral action, 'not according to the letter but according to the spirit',[8] the feeling of *movement and progression* has to find its means of expression. In the 'Caminhada' we find this as a significant sign of the religion of the people and one replete with new life. It is a *form of procession* in which the communual process is topically and typically directed to a common goal. The term 'procession' is avoided since it is strongly redolent of traditions associated with the official religion. There is the 'Caminhada' of repentance, and those of solidarity, of victory, of liberation, and of thanksgiving.

In the 'Caminhada of repentance', which takes place monthly in some places, the people of the quarter come together in order to process to church, while praying, singing and meditating. Before the church door the people of the parish ask for forgiveness and permission to enter. A distinction is made between the 'lesser' and the 'greater' Caminhada. Greater Caminhadas were held in the North East at the beginning of the rainy season after many years of drought. When the building of a church or chapel is complete, neighbouring parishes walk to the celebration in a Caminhada consisting of songs, spontaneous prayers and intervals for meditation. Reciprocal visits of this kind take place as forms of thanksgiving.

When *elections* were held under the military regime, the people spontaneously formed Caminhadas which went from the constitution square to the church and ended there with prayer and song. To what extent this form will be retained in the present process of democratisation cannot be assessed from the individualised election campaigns. The danger is not overlooked of the processions being taken over by politicians or a political party. Certainly what is required is an initial political situation of significance for all those taking part, such as undoubtedly exists at present in the demand for popular representation in a constitutive assembly (*Constituinte*).

Recently, in a city in the North East, on the occasion of the feastday of Judas Thaddeus, who also plays a part in the cults of African emphasis, two groups of faithful processed from their own districts to the Catholic parish church. One group contained members of the Candomblé cult, and included a 'Mãe-de-Santo' (priestess); the other group consisted of ecclesiastically oriented Christians. The two 'Caminhadas' met in front of the church and processed together to a service within. There were alternate petitions, and the impressive concluding prayer was recited by the 'Mãe-de-Santo'.

The past campaign against African cults and a deflection of people into the Umbanda cult are slowly giving way to a concern for *dialogue and encounter*. The multitude of African rites is seen as a possible means of enriching liturgical occasions. Fear of the possibility of a vulgar syncretism is still prevalent. Experiences from West Africa, for instance of funeral rites, are observed with interest.

4. PILGRIMAGES

Just as the 'Caminhada' injects religious life into and organises national space, the pilgrimage is a *spatial expression of a search for another religious reference-point*, one which leads away from itself to a religious centre. The reference framework of house, home and family is abandoned in order to discover a new religious source of life in the pilgrimage.[9] Here space and route play a large part. The North East of Brazil demands a special religio-geographical investigation in regard to the reciprocal relation of space and pilgrim/place of pilgrimage.

In contradistinction to the pilgrimages (Peregrinações) of official Church institutions for middle-class circles which go to Fatima in Portugal and all the way to the 'Holy Land', the pilgrimages known as 'romarias' are a *genuine expression of popular religion*.[10] The origin of the places of pilgrimage in the interior of Brazil usually derives from such popular needs, especially, for instance, in the 'Bandeirante cycle' of the seventeenth century, in the 'Mineiro cycle' of the eighteenth and in the 'Sertanejo cycle' of the last years of the eighteenth century all the way to the age of Romanisation in the nineteenth century.[11] Here, in addition to the images of saints or of Mary and Jesus, we have the images of popular saints, whether as hermits or as advisers (*conselheiro*) or 'healers', which have something of a crystallising function. The people themselves created and designed these religious centres. Two places of pilgrimage in the North East of Brazil have a supra-regional and indeed a national significance: Canindé with its cult of St Francis of the stigmata (São Francisco das Chagas) and Juazeiro with the cult of Our Lady of Dolours (Nossa Senhora das Dores) and the impressive figure of 'Padre Cícero'. Juazeiro was at first attacked by the Church hierarchy as a place of pilgrimage, was later tolerated, and is now accepted. This is connected with the figure of 'Padre Cícero'. which is scarcely accessible for the hierarchy. As a priest Cícero did much for the socio-economic and religious development of the very small place. Finally he was honoured by the people as their helper in all areas of life. A conflict with the hierarchy arose over the interpretation of a 'bleeding host'. A suspension from office was the result. Even then the people just could not understand why there were problems. For them the priest became a holy 'patriarch' deserving of the highest degree of respect. A *re-evaluation of his activities and effect* is slowly making way in ecclesiastical circles. The 'Centre for the Psychology of Religion' in Juazeiro offers the appropriate initial work and formation of consciousness. The popular publication 'How Father Cícero wanted to Fight Drought' was issued in association with the CNBB Service for Documentation and Popular Information of the regional group for the North East.[12] Religious psychological studies offer a differentiated picture of the pilgrimages to Juazeiro and the cult of Padre Cícero.[13]

5. CANINDE

The *pilgrimage centre* of Canindé is situated in the polygon of drought

(Polígono das Secas) in the North East of Brazil. A start was made on building a church in 1775, but it was only taken further after the drought years of 1777 and 1792 and finally completed in 1795, being dedicated to 'St Francis of the Stigmata'. Designed essentially for the needs of the area and the drought-plagued environment, with the installation of the large statue of St Francis in 1796 the church became a place of resort for the population of the larger environment in all their needs.

The cult of St Francis of the Stigmata, which derives from the influence of tertiaries of the Franciscan house in Recife, must have corresponded to the ideas and experiences of the suffering population. The condition of exposure to a nature which human beings cannot influence finds a meaningful reference-figure in the Francis who opened himself to God's grace. The idea of association with nature would seem to have been less influential than the birth and its accompanying legends and the blessed death of the saint.[14] The habit, or at least the *cingulum*, girdle, is carried nowadays on many pilgrimages as a symbol of repentance.

In the phase of Romanisation of Brazil, the brotherhood which administered the shrine was forced by an interdict (1888–1889) to surrender it to the diocese of Fortaleza. The diocese introduced Capuchins in 1898 and Franciscans from 1923 to care for the pilgrims pastorally. Financial administration remained with the diocese. The religious concerns of the Capuchins and Franciscans with regard to administration of the sacraments and preaching could count on the good will of the pilgrims. They wanted to honour their promises, to give thanks for favours granted and ask for grace. The word 'grace' (graça) is used by the pilgrims in addition to the term 'miracle'. Much may be read about miraculous favours on the votive tablets in the 'House of Miracles' (casa dos Milagres), which was built by the brothers. The countless 'ex-votos' refer to cures ascribed to St Francis of the Stigmata. To what extent the popular use here of the word 'grace' is the result of pressure from the official Church, or has arisen from a specific theology of the people, requires closer investigation. In spite of intensive pastoral efforts, above all during the festal period of October, when more than 100,000 pilgrims are assembled in the little town, some uncertainty is still discernible in members of the hierarchy. With constantly increasing numbers of pilgrims—there were half a million in 1985—those taking part and those responsible are faced with the question whether the forms and possibilities offered by the official Church can be approximated to the popular religion met with here.[15]

In 1985 recourse was had to 'Caminhadas' by the 44 chapel congregations roundabout. The intention was also to ensure religious participation at festal time of the very far-flung parish. The special masses for certain groups of faithful, such as drivers, farmers, cowboys (Vaqueiros) and singers (Violeiros) became more intensive. The active participation of the Archbishop of Fortleza, Cardinal Lorscheider, and his bishops was seen by the pilgrims as a form of encouragement.

The *Centre for Franciscan and Pastoral Studies in Latin America* (CEFE-PAL=centro de Estudos Franciscanos e Pastorais para a América Latina) has been holding annual courses in Canindé since 1979 under the symbolic title 'Mandacaru', which is an evergreen cactus of the drought-ridden North East. The religious who took part found listening to the voice of the faithful people and encounter with them increasingly meaningful. The option of the religious for the poor was reaffirmed. The people precipitated a learning process.[16]

The foundation of a 'Study Centre for the Popular Culture of Canindé' and the Second International Colloquium on the topic of 'Miracle Workers, Prophets and Healers: Faith, health, power', from 19–22 September 1985 at Canindé[17] show that other disciplines are showing interest and concern in investigating popular faith as a whole.[18]

CONCLUSION

Finally, I should like to offer some theses on popular religion, which an integral pastoral approach must take into account as a situational context:

1. Religion offers the people forms of thinking and statement in order to express their life-experiences in birth and death, natural events and suffering.

2. Social institutions are experienced as non-existent or ineffectual.

3. Experiences of suffering such as sickness, hunger, unemployment, and force represent a large number of the votive topics.

4. Relations to the sacred are experienced as forms of personal, affective contact which can also be expressed as disenchantment.

5. Divine justice is not questioned. Suffering is interpreted as trial or punishment.

6. Religion as a whole is conceived as a power which allows survival and resistance to cultural and political domination.

Translated by J.G. Cumming

Notes

1. See *Veja* (1.5.1985) 66.
2. *O São Paulo* (26.4.1986).

3. *Tribuna da Imprensa* (23.4.1985).

4. See *Jornal do Brasil* (13.4.1985).

5. Helcion ibeiro *Religiosidade Popular na Teologia Latino-Americana* (São Paulo 1981).

6. CNBB *Bibliografia sobre religiosidada popular: Estudos da CNBB* No. 27 (São Paulo 1981).

7. *Congregacõo para o Culto Divino: CNBB—comunicado Mensal 34 No. 392 (31.8.1985) 948.*

8. *Sebastião Armando G. Soares 'O Povo Biblioc. Referência para a nossa Caminhada—Cantar o Passado é anunciar o Futuro' in Perspectivas Teológico—Pastorais, Instituto de Teologia do Recife,* No. 1 (1985).

9. See E. Romer & A.A. Moles *Psychologie de l'Espace* (Brussels 1978); Murilo de Sa Barreto 'Ascese nas estradas em busca do Lugar Santo: A Vida em Cristo e na Igreja' in *Revista de Liturgia* No. 47 (1981).

10. See Pierre Sanchis 'Festa e Religião Popular—As Romarias de Portugal' in *Revista Vozes* No. 4 (May 1979) 279–294.

11. Riolando Azzi 'As Romarias no Brasil' in *Revista Vozes* No. 4 (May 1979) 279–294.

12. Centro de Psicologia de Religião/SEDIPO *Como Padre Cicero queria combater a Seca* (Juazeiro/Recife 1980).

13. A Dumoulin, T. Stella Guimarães 'Romaria em Juazeiro e a Devoccão ao Padre Cicero: A vida em Cristo e na Igreja' in *Revista de Liturgia* No. 65 (Sept.–Oct. 1984) 11–27.

14. V. Willecke *São Francisco dos Chagas de Canindé—Resumo Historico* (Canindé 1973) 2nd ed., pp 27ff.

15. M. Cantalice 'São Francisco de Canindé em 1980' in *Noticias da Provincia Franciscana de S. Antonio do Brasil* No. 10 (Oct. 1980) 5ff.

16. F. Schnittker *CEFEPAL—mandacaru, 4. Kursus, 12.-27.7-1984 in Canindé,* manuscript.

17. *Religião e Saúde* 'Profetas, Currandeiros e Taumaturgos: Fé, Saúde e Poder.'

18. See A. de Paula Barreto *La Médecine Populaire dans le Sertão du Ceará aujourd'hui* (Lyons 1985), manuscript.

Stephen Judd

Fashioning a Vital Synthesis: Popular Religion and the Evangelisation Project in Southern Peru

1. INTRODUCTION: EVANGELISATION, INCULTURATION AND POPULAR
RELIGION

ON THE eve of the twentieth anniversary of the closing of the Second Vatican Council, and the tenth anniversary of Pope Paul VI's apostolic exhortation, *Evangelii Nuntiandi*, it seems the appropriate moment for an evaluation and reflection on the evangelisation project in light of these two important turning points. In the context of Latin America, both the Medellín and Puebla Conferences captured the spirit of Vatican II and *Evangelii Nuntiandi*, and drew out the pastoral implications of those documents. At the same time, they broke new ground in tapping the rich theological vein that originated in Latin America.

As a result of these developments, interest has turned to a more careful consideration of the *theme of inculturation* here understood as 'the dynamic relation between the Christian message and culture or cultures; an insertion of the Christian life into a culture; an ongoing process of reciprocal and critical interaction and assimilation between them'.[1] In Latin America, talk of inculturation inevitably turns to a discussion of the merits of the phenomenon of *popular religion*. Puebla raised this issue to a new level of serious examination, although prior to the 1979 assembly, there was already a wealth of pastoral experience and reflection on which to draw.

The debate surrounding the Preparatory Document served to clarify the notion of culture, and the diversity of cultures and subcultures which give a unique expression to the Gospel in a number of different contexts and historical settings. In his critique of the Preparatory Document, *Gustavo*

Gutiérrez questions the idea of a homogeneous Latin American culture, and the presentation of popular religion 'as a bulwark of the traditional values betrayed by the secularist crisis'.[2] Moreover, he adds, the Latin American people is a Christian people, but it is also an exploited people. Within this duality we find the ambivalence of popular religiosity, but also its liberating potential.[3]

Evidence of the weight given to this critique and the response of several local churches is the Final Document itself which presents a much more nuanced and developed discussion of the theme. Thus, attempts at interpreting the theme popular religion in Puebla must be subject to the overall thrust of the document in its unequivocal statements on the option for the poor, its systematic analysis of the causes of poverty, and the important shift in viewing the poor as the subjects of evangelisation.

From a Gospel and Christological perspective, a key section of the Final Document is contained in paragraphs 31–39: 'This situation of pervasive extreme poverty takes on very concrete faces in real life. In these faces we ought to recognise the suffering features of Christ the Lord who questions and challenges us.' The text goes on to mention the faces of young children, indigenous peoples, peasants, the marginalised, etc., in an inspirational reflection that underlines the challenge of *'otherness'* as constitutive of the evangelisation project. These 'others' personalised in the *rostros* (faces) pose a challenge to long accepted categories of evangelisation. In the starkness of their poverty these insignificant 'others' resist any totalisation into our predetermined schemes. Understood in this way, popular religion, the religion of the poor, performs a transformative role becoming the interlocutor of what constitutes Christian identity.

The implications of this turn toward the 'others' as the subjects of evangelisation opens the way to a consideration of Puebla's more specific proposals on the challenge of popular religion. In order to authenticate the insights of Puebla, we present *a particular case study* of an evangelisation project in Peru wherein such a conversion process has been underway for centuries, and one that anticipated, to a great degree, the forward looking thrust of Puebla. This examination allows us the opportunity to explore further the challenge 'to fashion a vital synthesis from the Christian wisdom of the common people', and sets the stage for an 'appeal to the Christian memory of our peoples' (No. 448, 457).

2. EARLY EVANGELISATION AND THE DISCOVERY OF THE 'OTHERS'

The southern Andean departments of Puno and Cuzco inhabited by

Quechua and Aymara *campesinos* who trace their origins to the ancient civilisations which were later consolidated into the Inca Empire in the late fourteenth century, was the site of an important evangelisation effort from the time of the Spanish conquest in 1532 until roughly 1700. By one account, this evangelisation was achieved in *three successive stages*: an initial phase from 1540 to 1600 of intense missionary activity, followed by a period from 1600 to 1660 during which there were several campaigns to extirpate idols, and lastly the years 1660–1700, which shaped much of present day Peruvian belief and practice.[4] In this third stage, termed the 'cystallization period', autochthonous rituals, beliefs, festivals, and religious organisation merged with Spanish Catholicism, an amalgam of Counter-Reformation currents, popular folk piety, and influences inherited from Judaism and Islam.

Because of the persistence of Andean ritual forms, many scholars hold to the view of the existence of a dual religious system or syncretism. On the other hand, there are those who classify Andean Christianity as popular religion that derives from its rootedness in the life and worldview of the *campesino*, and distinguished it from the religion of élites who adhere to the worldview of Western Christianity.[5] From our standpoint, this view seems the most plausible one.

Whatever the case, we attribute this synthesis to a *remarkable evangelisation process* whereby the Gospel penetrated the ancient cultures despite the contradictions and violence associated with conquest. To no small degree, the genius and heroism of many of the early missionaries overcame their own zeal to win converts, and their appreciation of the values of the indigenous cultures allowed those cultures to *express the Gospel on their own terms*. Perhaps, in this initial stage, encounters with the 'other' contributed to the achievement of the vital synthesis. Noteworthy, in this respect, are figures of the stature of Bartolomé de Las Casas, whose peaceful method of conversion, his lifelong struggle against the evils of the *encomienda*, and his indefatigable defence of the rights of the Indians, extended to Peru. Likewise, the Jesuit evangelisation project in the Aymara speaking provinces of Puno, attests to an innovative approach whereby the indigenous peoples were considered as more than mere recipients of the deposit of the faith.

After the consolidation of colonial rule in the eighteenth century, and in the face of diminishing numbers of missionaries, evangelisation efforts were temporarily suspended. However, this development did not eclipse either the practice or the effect of Andean Christianity. New research into the Indian rebellions prior to and following independence in 1821, demonstrates the marked influence of religious sentiment as a motivating factor for popular leaders like Tupac Amaru in 1780.[6] Nineteenth century reformers, imbued with the ideas of Enlightenment philosophy and the influence of positivism, attempted to incorporate the indigenous peoples into the national life, but failed to recognise these peoples as 'others' with a distinct identity and cultural heritage. Later, massive seizures of Indian lands gave birth to the *hacienda* system and the continued exploitation of the indigenous peoples.

For the most part, the emergence of the so-called 'indigenista' movement of Peruvian intellectuals did little to ameliorate the condition of these peoples. Not until the 1920s with the writings of the philosopher and social thinker, José Carlos Mariátegui, did the *Indian emerge as the subject of history*, devoid of all romanticist conceptions. Mariátegui situated the problematic of the indigenous peoples within the scope of land ownership patterns, and the more structural inequities of Peruvian society.[7] Similarly, the novelist, José María Arguedas ascribed more of a protagonist role to the indigenous peoples and communities, not only in terms of their claims to autonomy, but as prime actors in the formation of a national consciousness. These developments laid the groundwork for the next stage of evangelisation in the southern Andes.

3. ACOMPANANDO A NUESTRO PUEBLO: A NEW MISSIONARY PRESENCE

The influx of North American and European missionaries beginning in the 1940s ushered in another stage of evangelisation. Whereas in some cases it was difficult for this new breed of missionary to level his or her perspective enough to resist the temptation to make over the 'other' into one's own image and likeness, there were definite signs of a *new opening to culture*. Developmentalist strategies and assistentialist projects notwithstanding, the promotion of lay catechists in the 1950s contributed to a heightened awareness of the 'other', especially when these local leaders were regarded as collaborators rather than auxiliaries.

Many of the area's bishops attended the sessions of Vatican II, and upon their return to Peru enthusiastically translated the spirit of documents like *Ad gentes* into practice. The establishment of research centres fostered ethnographic studies of the socio-cultural world of the Aymara and Quechua peoples, which in turn gave a new orientation to the pastoral work in the direction of a *more authentic inculturation*. Also, the learning of indigenous languages became a priority as well as the movement of pastoral agents to live and work in the countryside.

Due to the influence of the Medellín Conference and its espousal of a liberating evangelisation, *some of the emphases on cultural issues gave way to a concern for addressing the more pending structural problems* of the local and regional realities. When the failures of the reformist military government became apparent, notably in an insufficient land reform policy, coinciding with the first signs of organised popular discontent, the area's bishops responded with a series of bold pronouncements in solidarity with the popular classes.[8]

At the same time that the Church assumed the role of the 'voice of the voiceless', some observers noted the *shift away from the issue of inculturation.* Some attributed it to an awareness of the complexity of the issue.[9] On the other hand, some saw the cause of the shift in the critique that some pastoral agents were locked into a 'culturalista' bias to the neglect of the more conflictual factors affecting life in the countryside. Nevertheless, in taking a prophetic stand, the Church of the Sur Andino displayed a greater sensitivity to the suffering of the people. This shift would have far reaching consequences for the evangelisation project. Out of the experience of this local Church, in its posture of 'acompañando a nuestro pueblo' (accompanying our people), popular religion came to be regarded *not only as a feature of the people's identity, but as a factor in the transformation of society.* At massive celebrations and convocations, in a broader vision of lay leadership and an expanded role for the *campesino* in the construction of a local church, and in a more coordinated plan of evangelisation, the Church of the South Andes demonstrated the potential to respond in a more creative way to the challenges of Puebla concerning popular religion.

4. THE PROBLEM OF THE LAND AND THE FEAST OF THE CROSS

Unquestionably, in the Anean world, the relationship between the *campesino* and the land is not only based on its productive capacity, but herein is contained a bond of great symbolic meaning. This bond persists in spite of the less than promising future for the *campesino* community. Climatological factors as well as the negligence of the successive governments' agrarian policies make subsistence farming a precarious enterprise. One inevitable result is an intensification of migration to the coastal cities, depleting valuable human resources. In the face of these developments, the independent *campesino* organisations press even more urgently for a just distribution of the land. At stake, too, is the future of the *campesino* community, a *symbol of bondedness to the land.*

During the drought of 1982–84, the Church was able to sense more deeply the entire problematic, and to enter into the process of a sobering reflection over future alternatives. More significantly, pastoral workers were awed by the resiliency of the people to respond to the crisis with renewed hope. In the midst of the crisis, the celebration of religious rites and festivals took on a greater significance.

For the outsider, the ritual life of Andean peoples organised in accordance with the Christian liturgical calendar, but celebrated according to the rhythms of the agricultural cycle, highlights the distinctiveness of Andean Christianity. Therein lies our starting point for a reflection on the beginnings of a *local theology*. Based on our earlier assumption that we discover Christ in the 'faces' of the poor, we move to a *consideration of these festivals celebrated in the context of the social situation described above*. Following the criteria outlined by Robert Schreiter in his study on the construction of local theologies, with this selection we touch upon a point in the Andean cultures where 'tension and ill are most strongly felt'.[10]

A recent survey on popular religion in Peru concludes 'that the cross in its diverse forms and its undeniable reference to the passion of Christ constitutes the symbolic nucleus of Peruvian popular religion'.[11] So, too, in the Andean context, the *cross* occupies a central place in popular devotions as well as in the ritual cycle generating a surplus of meanings in an ever changing and fluid social situation. This convergence points us in the direction of a fuller understanding of the paschal implications not so readily accessible to the outsider. Thus, these Andean *fiestas* become our 'texts' for discovering the elements of a local theology.

According to Curt Cadorette, in the Aymara world there is an *intensity in the Holy Week celebrations* that offers a contrast,—and a more convincing insight into the paschal mystery—with Western observances: 'What seems implicit in the perspective of the Aymara *campesino* about Jesus and his redemption is the idea that without assimilating the same suffering, and without passing through the same sense of abandonment, any declaration of faith is essentially a euphemism.'[12]

For example, in the town of Moho on the north side of Lake Titicaca, the Good Friday celebration presents a reenactment of a ceremony with roots in medieval Spain. The *piadosos*, a fraternity of men from the community who dress in white robes, enter the church on Good Friday and proceed to lift the life size statue of the body of Christ from the cross. After cleansing his body with hundreds of small pieces of perfumed cotton, the statue, now in a glass encased coffin, is carried out in procession through the streets. At the conclusion of the procession, the cotton is distributed to those assembled. The highly coveted pieces of cotton are kept in the home for protection. When sickness or disaster strike, they are burned and placed into a medicinal tea. In this way, the bond of identification with the crucified Christ is actualised and kept alive. Until recently, when the pastoral agents invited the participants of this ritual back into the church building, this centuries old ritual was celebrated clandestinely on the outskirts of town.

Where the cross takes on an even greater paschal significance is during the *Feast of the Exaltation of the Cross* on 14th September, and *the Feast of the Finding of the True Cross* on 3rd May. The exaltation of the cross is celebrated in springtime at the start of the planting season. Any semblance of somberness disappears in the frenzied swirl of colourful dances and decorative crosses. Instead of reflections on the mystery of Christ's suffering and death, the prayers of the people invoke the protection of the cross in anticipation of the long growing season when their fields are susceptible to frosts and hail.

In May there is an even more pronounced air of festivity when the fiesta becomes the occasion for celebrating the first fruits of the harvest. In an area where bountiful harvests are the exception, the thanksgiving motif reinforces the *campesino's* awareness of the gifted quality of the land. Decorative crosses in every community depict the joy of another year's harvest. The paschal implications are all too obvious.

All of these *fiestas are celebrated in a massive fashion*—with processions and pilgrimages—bringing together all sectors of the community, and are marked by the return of former residents who renew bonds of friendship as well as affirm their allegiance to their native land. At Puebla, the Church underlined the importance 'of the religious expressions of the common people *en masse* for the evangelising force that they possess' (No. 467). These elements of thanksgiving, fraternity and reunion evangelise the pastoral agent as well as strengthen the cohesiveness of the *campesino* community.

In so far as there are traces of a *liberation motif*, they are contained in the very fact of the uninterrupted observance and celebration of the fiesta of the cross. According to Diego Irarrázabal, 'out of this live tradition—and not from introducing any "liberating ideas"—a liberating evangelisation takes place'.[13] 'This storehouse of values that offers the answers of Christian wisdom to the great questions of life' presents the pastoral agent with a vast array of challenges. Perhaps, here, we glimpse the outlines of a local theology more in tune with the wisdom tradition as suggested by Schreiter.[14]

Still unanswered, however, is the *absence of a historical dimension, and a clearer Christological reference in terms of discipleship*. How does one, following Puebla, 'make an appeal to the Christian memory of our peoples'? In this context, what kind of pedagogy would best serve to encourage a more explicit reflection on the significance communicated through these rites and fiestas? How do we appraise in a critical way changes in the celebration that prefigure a more individualistic motivation behind the fiesta? We offer *some tentative approaches* to answer these questions.

By virtue of the bonds of confidence and solidarity already established, the pastoral agent in his or her insertion into the Andean world described above, enjoys a *privileged mode of entry*. In fact, there is already an ongoing dialogue initiated in the encounter with the 'other' that elicits responses from the pastoral agent who does not arrive at the encounter empty-handed. Rather, he or she has already demonstrated the capacity to become what Otto Maduro, in a variation of the Gramscien notion of the organic intellectual, calls 'a religious functionary spontaneously sought out by the masses for the purpose of gathering, systematising, expressing, and making response to the aspirations and needs of these subordinate classes'.[15]

Concretely applied to our context, the systematising task involves a *listening and a dialogue* with the people over the history of the fiesta and the devotion of the cross. How was this fiesta celebrated during the *campesino* rebellions of the early part of this century? What does it signify in the present crisis, and our claims to a just redistribution of the land? How do we draw strength from this devotion? In our conflictual reality, what are the consequences of taking up one's cross and following Jesus? These are among the questions that surface in the type of dialogue we are proposing, and that would hopefully lead us to a recovery of 'Christian memory' as well as foster a project aimed at a mutual evangelisation.

5. CHALLENGES: INCULTURATION AND 'INCURABLE OTHERNESS'

When Puebla reached its conclusions on the question of popular religion, different local churches had at their disposal a *wealth of experience*, and ongoing evangelisation projects that directly addressed, albeit incompletely, the issues of inculturation. Churches like that of the Sur Andino anticipated the insights of Puebla. Past and present efforts were both affirmed and challenged. Yet, it has become apparent that there are *still great strides to be made*. Puebla and the subsequent theological reflection in Latin America point the way to a recovery of 'the Christian memory of our peoples', and supply the energy and resources for fashioning a 'vital synthesis out of the Christian wisdom of our people'.

Drawing upon this vast storehouse of living testimonies along with the values of popular religion, Latin America fulfills its mission to evangelise other local churches 'out of our own poverty'. That poverty expresses itself through the questioning 'other', our interlocutor, who in the words of the

Spanish poet Antonio Machado, 'refuses to disappear, who subsists, who persists; the incurable otherness from which oneness must always suffer.'[16]

Notes

1. M. Carvalho Azevedo *Inculturation and the Challenges of Modernity* (Rome 1982) p. 11.
2. Gustavo Gutiérrez *The Power of the Poor in History* (New York 1983)p. 123.
3. *Ibid.* p. 123.
4. Manuel Marzal *La transformación religiosa peruana* (Lima 1983).
5. Henrique Urbano 'Representaciones colectivas y arquelogía mental en los Andes' *Allpanchis* 20 (1982).
6. Jeffrey Klaiber *Relgion and Revolution in Peru, 1824–1976* (Notre Dame, Indiana 1977). Also see Klaiber's article 'Religión y justicia en Tupac Amaru' *Allpanchis* (19) 1982.
7. José Carlos Mariátegui *Seven Interpretive Essays on Peruvian Reality* (Austin, Texas 1971).
8. *Acompañando a nuestro pueblo: Iglesia del Sur Andino* (1978).
9. José Luis Gonzalez *En el corasón de su pueblo, dos obispos del Sur Andino* (Lima, Peru 1982).
10. Robert Schreiter *Constructing Local Theologies* (New York 1985) p. 74.
11. José Luis Gonzalez *La religiosidad popular en el Perú* (Lima,Peru 1984) p. 65.
12. Curt Cadorette 'Perspectivas mitológicas del mundo aymara' *Boletín del Instituto de Estudios Aymaras* (August 1979) 16.
13. Diego Irarrazabal La cruz de un pueblo crucificado' *Pastoral Popular* 15 (1981) 15.
14. Schreiter, the work cited in note 10, at pp. 85–87.
15. Otto Maduro *Religion and Social Conflicts* (New York, 1982) p. 144.
16. Quoted in preface of Octavio Paz *The Labyrinth of Solitude* (New York 1961).
NOTE: All quotes from the Final Document of Puebla are taken from the English translation, *Puebla and Beyond* ed. Eagleson and Scharper (New York 1979).

Paulo Suess

The Creative and Normative Role of Popular Religion in the Church

THE POPULAR religious practices found in the Church in Latin America, are in the Nahuatl saying, 'flowers' and songs', 'true words of wisdom' rising up from the ruins of the Conquest and which somehow 'escaped from its final destruction'.[1] These *popular religious practices*—called by a variety of names in the Puebla final document[2]—have over the course of history *been treated with a mixture of persecution and selective acceptance by the ministers of official religion.* The few efforts at missionary inculturation with the indigenous peoples have overall left no historical traces. The aim of such inculturation was rather a Catholic Church among the Indians than a properly indigenous Church.

In the *colonial Church*, which in Latin America dated from pre-Tridentine times, lay people played a major role and religious practices therefore enjoyed a large measure of autonomy. The faith of the people, living a long way from the churches and from clerical ministrations, revolved round devotion to saints of the homestead or locality; it showed itself in vows, processions and festivals. With the saints, the crucified Christ is still the inspiration for the great pilgrimages. The function of the clergy in this colonial Christendom, who saw themselves as representatives of true Catholicism—traditional Iberian Catholicism, that is—in the face of these 'outlandish customs', was reduced to saying mass and administering the sacraments.[3]

Starting only in the *middle of the nineteenth century*, 'reforming' bishops struggled to implant the reforms of Trent, control of the clergy and of popular religion, and independence from State control and patronage. When Brazil became a Republic in 1889, Church and State were separated, which led to an increase in this process of Romanising the Catholic Church. The Holy See sent endless religious congregations to the Mission fields, and virtually till the time of Vatican II they took their pastoral approach from their European backgrounds. 'Apostolic missions' (to the Mapuche tribes of Indians), annual visits (in Amazonia) and 'holy missions' (in the cities) attempted to remedy 'religious ignorance' and to tighten the institutional bonds between popular and official religion.

In Spain, the fourteen bishops of the provinces of Seville and Granada produced a document, 'New pastoral considerations on popular Catholicism', on 20 February 1985. In this they point to its revitalisation in Southern Spain, particularly in 'the Holy Week celebrations, pilgrimages and feasts of patron saints'. They claim that 'true Christian faith is present in popular Catholicism', but give serious warnings about its manipulation by political, economic and religious influences. In particular they speak—in surprising accord with Puebla (455, 456, 914)—of 'lack of proper concern on the part of official representatives', of 'holy terror', 'ritualistic obsession', 'magical excesses', and censure the 'over-valuation of devotion to the dead and the saints'.

The high religious temperature of the people in general—in Andalusia 85% called themselves believing Catholics—is in contrast with a rather stagnant eucharistic practice. Belonging to the Church is a matter of popular religion and not of regular frequentation of the sacraments. In their dossier 'Andalusia. Report to John Paul II', the authors speak of Sunday mass attendance of around 15%.[4] The remedies suggested by these fourteen bishops are those universally applied in the Church, from *Evangelii nuntiandi* (48) and *Catechesi Tradendae* (54): 'a pedagogy of evangelisation' and 'adequate catechesis'. Puebla speaks of 'constantly evangelising over again' (457). While the document warns against the 'possible manipulation of various tendencies' in popular Catholicism, it insists on the *safeguarding* and *promotion* of its values.

In view of the continuous and mainly unsuccessful efforts of the universal Church to integrate all peoples into a liturgy of supposed universality, *Gaudium et Spes* recognised the *need for inculturation*, since the Church 'from the beginning of her history . . . has learned to express the message of Christ with the help of the ideas and terminology of various peoples' (44a). It is a constant fact of history that a non-inculturated Church always places popular religion in danger of paganism, heresy or syncretism. Incarnation in the culture of 'others' and in the social class of the 'poor and simple people'

(EN 48) overturns the neo-colonial perspective of integration and extension. Inculturation in the life of the people could be the Church's most significant contribution to their liberation, whether in Andalusia, Amazonia or the Andes.

Popular religion is a *manisfestation of popular culture*, conferring the coherence of an overall vision on the whole gamut of social practices. It is also a cultural system of communication, using symbolical practices and interpretation. Just as every spoken language develops historically, imposing changing speech patterns (popular) on grammatical conventions (official), so too the religion experienced by the people is modelled by a creative force originating in the orchestration of their social conditions and contradictions with their historical consciousness forged in their struggle for life. The socio-historical sources of popular religion produce changes in the religious rules of the game, in symbolical meaning, in socio-political consciousness and in religious practice. The relative autonomy of the religious field, which keeps the faith of the people safe from sacralisation or political ideology, lends popular religious practices a very strong power of *alternative socio-political mobilisation.*

The *popular* notion of popular religion, as understood here, does not embrace the religious feeling of the whole 'people of God', identified with the Church or even the totality of religious practices of a whole people or nation. This is the populist 'vision' of popular religion, which abstracts an idea of the 'good people' in order to cover over the contradictions in society. Like its condemnation by ethnocentric rationalism, populist idealisation of popular religion deprives the people of their historical character and prevents them from becoming subjects of their own destiny. Those who only fight for the cause of 'good people' do not go far in solidarity. Popular religion is, normally, the *religious expression of the poor*, lay people who live on the margins of the dominant imported culture. And just as women play an important part in popular culture and struggles, so they came to the fore in popular religion, questioning the patriarchal *machismo* of Latin America and its ideological support in a platonic Mariology.

When certain symbols and popular religious practices are *appropriated by the ruling classes*, they lose their popular significance and become a part of what goes to make up 'traditional religiosity', an instrument of symbolical manipulation in the interest of outside powers. Where the 'poor and simple people' fail to understand that they are being manipulated in this way, popular religion becomes a factor of alienation. How can one explain the continued presence of 'structures of sin' on the Latin American continent except as partly through the accommodation of popular religion to structures of domination? (Puebla, 452) Looking at the exuberance of some religious festivals, the luxury of the processional trappings and the excessive austerity of some penitential practices, who would dare to point to the exact position of the dividing line between popular longing for a new world and imitation of the old world of the rich? True popular religious practices are always those of a people made up of 'saints and sinners', involved in the advances, setbacks and dreams of a particular historical moment.

The *religious authority of the Church*, its structures and doctrine, are today being *questioned* on the basis of the parameters of its human competence. On this continent, it is not only its widespread Catholicism that is a constant feature; its premature deaths and overall poverty are equally widespread. This 'believing people', in the great majority of Latin American countries, lives in 'a situation of extreme poverty' (Puebla 31), on the borders of life. The people's access to the means of salvation is hindered not only by the complacency of official religion, but also by barriers within it. How does one reconcile 'basic' pronouncements of Vatican II, such as 'No Christian community, however, can be built up unless it has its basis and centre in the celebration of the most holy Eucharist' (PO 6), with the restrictive practice represented by the existence of a virtual ministerial 'closed shop'?

The *polarity between popular and official religion* is a phenomenon tied to the context of a classist society and to the hierarchical mediations of monotheism. It is the tension between the universality of a God for all and the particularity of the cultural setting, social class and historical period. Popular religion is not just a degraded form of official religion, just as life is not merely an application of theoretical principles. The religious practices of the popular classes produce an original wisdom. Revelation projected on to the screen of the life of the poor generates a decisive understanding of how to transform this world and install the Kingdom. This understanding, however, can find itself discounted by the Church—by its theology and its *magisterium*—can fall by the wayside. Official and popular religion are mutually dependent on their *reciprocal reception*. Non-reception of popular creativity produces frustrations of hope within the Church, which contrast sadly with the hope experienced along with the feelings of solidarity and fraternal love found in the midst of the people.

The evangelisation carried out by the popular classes—the people continually evangelise themselves (Puebla 450)—is done on the continuing basis of their *reading of reality in the light of the word of God*. In Latin American today, the poor have really taken over the word of God, re-reading in community the events that formed the people of God. *Practice of reciprocal evangelisation between popular and official religion* guarantees that, in the first place, official religion does not become a hierarchy without a people, ministering a doctrine without life, while for its part, popular religion does not turn into just another sect. An official religion in the service of the poor and their religious practices—an 'organic' religion, in Gramsci's sense of the word—will never live with popular religion in complete freedom from conflict; it will, however, reduce the false dialectic between 'basism' and 'vanguardism' to a tension between poles that can generate light for both. If they are organically interwoven, both popular and official religion can produce their witnesses, learned in and zealous for the faith.

The 'poor and believing' people—primary recipients of the Good News— do not represent *the* Church or *the* people of God exclusively within the overall framework of the universal Church. Likewise, the religious practices of these people do not represent the only sort of religious practice that is legitimate within the Catholic Church, where there should be room for *different cultural expressions*, provided these do not represent classes in conflict. A community of Benedictine monks will express its praise of God in a legitimately different way from a base community in the middle of Amazonia. The normative strength of popular religion cannot consist in imposing *one* form of popular religion on the whole Church from below: like replacing the liturgy of the Roman Church, for example, with *a* liturgy devised for *one* culture of povety. The normative power of popular religion does, however, involve *breaking the monopoly of one universal liturgy*, whose 'implantation' in the Third World has come about through literal translations and folkloric adaptations of indigenous cultures. Popular religion, 'with moving fervour and purity of intention' (CT 54), will—in the long run—make the Church a place where a Pentecostal plurality of tongues becomes the normal way of praising God. Such a *plurality* will not represent an isolationist autonomy, but reflect the variety of religious practices within the Church. The 'creative dynamism' of popular religion will serve 'to incarnate the universal prayer of the Church in our culture in a greater and better way' (Puebla 465), provided we do not allow a liturgical apartheid to creep into the City of God, with a 'white' minority laying down the law for the wretched of the earth.

Since Tyrus Prosperus of Aquitaine—a lay monk and pupil of St Augustine, who died in 455—it has been the tradition of the Church that the people's practice of prayer constitutes, in a certain sense, the practice of the faith.[5] But if the due creativity and plurality of religious practices is to be assured, not every prayer, liturgy or religious practice is to be considered *de fide*. Furthermore, popular religion, which is basically a lay religion inscribed in the culture of the poor, reveals an authentic *sensus fidelium*, not only on a subjective and individual basis, but originating collectively and remaining a collective possession. In the Church, lay people are the specific recipients of revelation. Christ fulfills his prophetic office 'not only through the hierarchy . . . but also through the laity', for which purpose he gave them 'understanding of the faith and the grace of speech' (LG 35). There exists also in the Catholic Church a long doctrinal tradition of the infallibility of the people in matters of faith.[6] This infallibility 'in credendo' cannot be exercised against the infallibility 'in docendo' of the magisterium, since the subjects of the magisterium themselves make up part of 'the body of the faithful as a whole', which 'cannot err in matters of belief' (LG 12). But the infallibility in docendo always includes a 'consensus fidelium'—an objective and communitary understanding of faith—embracing all '"from the bishops down to the last member of the laity"' (LG 12, quoting St Augustine). Infallibility in credendo and in docendo only pass into the history of the Church through the action of their practical and reciprocal reception. In Church administration, however, 'popular infallibility' has always been frustrated by the structures and exercise of power. The present ministerial set-up minimises lay participation in the magisterium, which is envisaged by the paradigm of infallibility in credendo.

Recognition of lay people by the magisterium would still not, in itself, allow proper space for the normative and creative role of popular religion in the Church, unless the mechanics of its choice of and adherence to the 'poor and simple' were made plain. The doctrine of sensus fidelium, with its hierarchical safeguards and rather vague reference to the 'body of the faithful as a whole', does not in practice get us much beyond a theoretical recognition of certain 'human rights' or basic principles in the Church. There is a difference when we come to the traditional teaching on the 'order or "hierarchy" of truths', which Vatican II took up in the Decree on Ecumenism (11). In the symphony of faith, there is an 'order or "hierarchy" of truths', in which not all sounds have the same duration or volume or value. Some pick out the melody, others mark the beat, others are mere grace notes. And this applies not only to relations with 'separated brethren'; it also applies to approaches to the 'poor and simple'. The periphery of the poor have their own mediations and make their own specific reading of the requirements of the Kingdom of God. In their religious practices, the poor offer 'the answers of Christian wisdom to the great questions of life' (Puebla 448). This wisdom is also a 'principle of discernment' (ibid.); it is a popular understanding of faith, an operational sensus fidelium, because it has a socio-cultural and historical context. Popular wisdom—which 'bears . . . the seal of the heart and its intuitions' (414)—is a 'vital synthesis', capable of withstanding attempts to divide 'the divine and the human . . . spirit and body . . . person and community . . . intelligence and emotion' (448—against 914!). Forged in suffering, the wisdom of the poor establishes a 'hierarchy of truths' in relation to their basic necessities of life. In a general way, dogmatic deviations are not found in popular religion, but reflections of a social scandal are. Recognition of the 'hierarchy of truths' of the poor and of the normative character of popular religion in the Church is not so much a doctrinal matter as a question of *power structures, understanding, or conversion.*

The 'social contract' of a nation and the 'world view' of a people presuppose *options*—not always conscious—based *a priori* not on scientific reasoning but on consensus. Consensus as a collective option springs from a new understanding responding to a new historical situation and need. So Puebla's 'clear and prophetic option expressing preference for, and solidarity with, the poor' (1134) is not something opportune or 'optional' in relation to the content of faith. The option for the poor does not represent a possible division of labour between the churches of the Third and First Worlds. The 'evangelising potential of the poor' (1147) calls for 'constant conversion and purification among all Christians' (1140). The emergence of the poor as subjects of history is a sign of the times, perceived—like all God's signs in time—far sooner and more clearly on the periphery of humanity than in the centre. Puebla's option bears the stamp of human urgency and evangelical necessity, because God opted decisively for the poor long before the churches did.

The central religious experience of the *people of Israel* was the *experience of one God*, who made an alliance with his people and set them free. In the geographical centre of this experience, half way along the road from the land of slavery to the promised land, on Mount Sinai, the people of God put down the roots of their worship, in which they looked forward to a new society, rebuilt their origins and projected their future. The God of the Alliance, who set his people free, is the God who made earth and life; he is also the God of the 'new creation'. Liberation redeems creation from the corruption of sin. The people of Israel recognised their creator God in the *experience of liberation.* This God of the Alliance, creator and liberator, *sent his son*—with no place in which to be born (Luke 2:7), with no place to lay his head (Matt. 8:20) and with no place in which to be buried (Matt. 27:60)—to proclaim a Good News to the poor (Luke 4:18). His place in the world was on the road, the place of the poor. The carpenter's son from Nazareth, incarnated in a particular social class and cultural setting, who 'became our brother, poor like us' (Puebla 1145), showed the coherence of his teaching in his works. Popular religion finds the basis for its norms in the works of Jesus who, besides working 'magic' in curing the woman with an issue of blood, recognised her act of faith, who nevertheless did not hesitate to expel the traders from the temple and who instructed the scribe in the love that was 'far more important than any holocaust or sacrifice' in the temple (Mark 5:34; 11:15; 12:33). *Jesus purified the religious practices of his people on his way* and opened up new and broader horizons of hope and solidarity. These people always on the road—processions and pilgrimages are some of the most pertinent expressions of popular religion—have a historical mission and an eschatological mission to fulfil, because they are used by God 'as an instrument for the redemption of all' (LG 9). The prophetic and messianic people of the poor are sent to the world to be its light and leaven. The universal liberation of the cosmos, the installation of the 'new heaven and new earth' will be mediated through the active creativity and universal liberation of the poor.

Even before Puebla, the *universal Church had opted explicitly for the poor.* It took on the hopes and griefs 'especially of those who are poor' (GS 1); it recognised 'in the poor and suffering the likeness of (its) poor and suffering Founder' (LG 8); it accepted that 'the Church must walk the same road which Christ walked: a road of poverty and obedience, of service and self-sacrifice to the death, from which death he came forth a victor by his resurrection' (AG 5). The poor thereby became a new *locus* for theological work, a situation in which the theological virtues are experienced with a fervent density of life. Their religious practices, besides being a legitimate 'expression of Catholic *faith*' (Puebla 444), contain in their 'cry for true liberation' (452), the 'expectation (*hope*) of a new earth' (GS 39). The 'poor and simple' people carry out all their earthly activities 'in one vital synthesis with religious values' (GS 43); they make their *love* for their neighbour and for God concretely present in acts of fraternity, of solidarity, of service and availability (Puebla 448, 1147).

By its option for the poor, the Church formally *renounced the dominant religious role it played in Christendom.* In their religious practices, the poor call into question the power structures and economic conditions that sustain the theological discourse of official religion. They challenge the ideological interpretation of the socio-cultural differences between official and popular religion which would make the former evangelically superior. Sophisticated zeal for the contents of faith, disconnected from the primary recipients of the Gospel, and badly communicated through the dominant culture inhibits any creative capacity coming from the people. It is not possible in the Church to opt for the poor and at the same time exclude their manner of religious expression from this option, or try to codify it with 'cerebral curiosity for the chemistry of faith or anatomy of belief'.[7]

Vatican II's introduction of vernacular languages for the liturgy, for example, was a sign not to continue with a transposition or literal translation of the rites or liturgy of the ruling classes, but to put the celebrations of faith in the Church into the *language of the people*. Authoritarian vigilance over universal application of a single liturgy prevents 'the religion of the people, with its symbolic and expressive richness, (from providing) the liturgy with creative dynamism' (Puebla 465). Puebla states that 'the crux of liberative evangelisation . . . is to transform human beings into active subjects' (485). In this logic of the people as *integral subjects*, 'the people's religious life is not just an object of evangelisation' (450). If the Church really intends to play the part proper to it in this task of evangelisation or catechising, then it must, on a universal scale—rather than increase the frequency or number of its communications—unblock the channels of communication. This requires a *redoubled effort to inculturate the message and celebration of faith* in the religious and social practices of the people. In its proximity to the poor, the Church finds the parameters for the inculturation and purification of its own religious expression. In 'the Church of the poor', in the words of John Paul II, the universal Church confirms 'its fidelity to Christ' (*Laborem Exercens* 8)

The *normative nature* of popular religion is rooted in the normative force of following Christ, who became poor in order to be and to announce the Good News to the poor. In the option for the poor, the religious and social practices of the Church—its religious nature and poverty—are taken up into the missionary horizon of salvation and universal liberation. This option is the proclamation of a *new social identity for a Church* which declares itself a universal servant Church 'that prolongs down the ages Christ, the servant of Yahweh, by means of its various ministries and charisms' (Puebla 1303). Being 'taken up into' means being closely bound up with, but not identified with or disappearing into.[8] The critical and organic relationship between popular and official religion preserves faith from ideological reduction and from being sacralised in a particular historical project. The poor not only see the signs of the times more clearly, because they feel them in their flesh; they also last longer than any manifestation of partisan politics.

The *voiceless and homeless*, those dumb seekers after utopia in the socio-political field, have *won recognition* of the normative role of their religious voice and their theological place *in* the Church by the 'option' *of* the Church. The poor who become the political subjects of their own destiny will not accept being patronised in religious matters. Besides, in religious matters the poor have never lacked a voice: 'if these keep silence the stones will cry out' (Luke 19:40). But there have been times in the Church when the frequency on which their voice goes out has been received distortedly or only by a few. Neither the socio-religious practices of the saints, nor those of the poor, have always corresponded to the official ecclesiastical options of their time. The speech of the poor requires changes to be made in the official grammars and dictionaries, in a collaborative venture of evangelical discernment. The dynamism and mysticism of the road trod by the poor challenge the a-historical 'stations' taken up by the Church. In the name of life, the poor are indissolubly bound up in change. They are committed to the Kingdom of God, which chooses to be praised 'by the mouths of children' (Ps. 8:1) and which calls the little ones to change the world and convert the Church.

Translated by Paul Burns

Notes

1. M. Léon-Portilla *La filosofia nahuatl estudiada en sus fontes* (Mexico 1983) p. 145.

2. The Conclusions of the Third General Conference of Latin American Bishops in 1979, published as *Puebla* (Washington D.C., Slough & London, 1980), use the terms 'religion of the people', 'popular religiosity', 'popular piety', 'popular Catholicism', 'religiosity of the people' and 'popular religion' virtually interchangeably—see 444, 452, 455 etc. We have here stuck to the expression 'popular religion'. There is a good account of current work on the question in H. Ribeiro *Religiosidade popular na teologia latino-americano* (São Paulo 1985).

3. See R. Azzi *O episcopado do Brasil frente ao catolicismo popular* (Petrópolis 1977) p. 114.

4. See M. Roman 'La evangelización en Andalucía, hoy' in *Vida nueva* 1492 (1985) 23–30.

5. 'De gratia Dei indiculus' c. 8, in PL 51, 209ff: ('legem credendi lex statuat supplicandi').

6. See G. Thils 'L'Infaillibilité du peuple chrétien *in credendo*' in *Bibl. Ephem. Theol. Lovan.*, XXI (1963).

7. L. da Camara Cascudo *Supersticão no Brasil* (São Paulo 1985) p. 394.

8. See Pope John XXIII *Princeps Pastorum* 13; LG 13; GS 22 and 58; AG 22; EN 20: *Puebla* 400 and 469.

Contributors

JEAN DELUMEAU was born in Nantes in 1923, entered the E.N.S. in 1943, was a member of the Ecole française de Rome between 1948-1950, became reader, then professor of modern history at Rennes between 1955-70, then professor of modern history in Paris I between 1970-75. He was director of studies at the EPHE (6th section) between 1963-78, and has been associate director at the EHESS since 1978. He has been professor at the Collège de France since 1975. He gained the Grand Prix de l'Académie Française in 1968 for *La Civilisation de la Renaissance*; the Grand Prix des écrivains catholiques in 1977, the Grand prix d'Histoire de la Ville de Paris in 1981 and the Médaille d'or de la municipalité de Rome in 1985. His publications include *Vie économique et sociale de Rome dans la seconde moitié du XVI siècle* (1957-59); *L'Alun de Rome* (1962); *Naissance et affirmation de la Réforme* (1965); *La Civilisation de la Renaissance* (1967); *Le Catholicisme entre Luther et Voltaire* (1971); *L'Italie de Botticelli à Bonaparte* (1974); *Le Christianisme va-t-il mourir?* (1977); *La Peur en Occident (XIVe-XVIIIe siècles): Une cité assiegée* (1978); *Histoire vécue du peuple chretien* (under his direction) (1979); *Un Chemin d'histoire* (1981); *Le Péché et la peur. La culpabilisation en Occident* (XIIIe-XVIIIe siècles) (1983); *Le Cas Luther* (1983); *Ce que je crois* (due to appear).

ENRIQUE DUSSEL is an Argentine and a Catholic and lives in Mexico. He holds doctorates in philosophy (Madrid 1959) and history (Sorbonne 1967) and an honorary doctorate in theology (Freiburg 1981). He is professor of ethics in the Autonomous University of Mexico and of Church history and theological method in ITES (Mexico). He is president of the Church history commission (CEHILA) and coordinator of the same commission in EATWOT (the Ecumenical Association of Third World Theologians). Among his writings are *A History of the Church in Latin America* (1981); *Philosophy of Liberation* (1985); *Etica comunitaria* ('Community Ethics'), in the collection 'Theology and Liberation' (1986) (English, German and French translations in preparation).

VIRGIL ELIZONDO, Ph.D., S.T.D. was born in San Antonio, Texas

(U.S.A.) and studied at the Ateneo University (Manila); at the East Asian Pastoral Institute (Manila); and at the Institut Catholique (Paris). Since 1971, he has been president of the Mexican American Cultural Center in San Antonio. He has published numerous books and articles; been on the editorial board of *Concilium, Catequesis Latino Americana* and of the *God with us* Catechetical Series, Sadlier Publishers, Inc. (U.S.A.). He does a great deal of theological reflection with the grass-roots people in the poor neighborhoods of the U.S.A.

OSMAR ERWIN GOGOLOK, OFM., was born in Friedenshütte, Upper Saxony, Germany, in 1933. He is a member of the Franciscan province of North-Eastern Brazil of St Antony, Recife. He was ordained priest in 1959. He studied German language and literature, philosophy and geography. Director of the Brazilological Institute, Mettingen. Editor of the journal *Brasilien-Dialog*. He has published: *Slums im Nordosten Brasiliens. Favelas als Stadt-geographisches Problem* (Mettingen 1980).

ERNEST HENAU was born in 1937 at Erwetegen, Belgium. He became a Passionist in 1956 and was ordained priest in 1963. He was awarded his doctorate in theology by the Catholic University of Louvain in 1967 and has taught in the theological faculties of that University and of Tilburg. In 1975–76 he worked at the A. von Humboldt-Stiftung of the University of Wurzburg in the Federal Republic of Germany. He is at present professor of Pastoral Theology at the University for Theology and Pastoral Work at Heerlen in the Netherlands. His most important writings include *Waarom kerk?* (1974); *Inleiding tot de praktische homiletiek* (1976); *God is groter* (1980), in collaboration with J. Beers; *Verscheidenheid en kerkbetrokkenheid* (1982).

STEPHEN JUDD, M.M., was born in Butte, Montana (USA) in 1945. He received a B.A. degree in Spanish from the University of Montana, and a M.A. in Latin American literature from the University of New Mexico. After receiving a Master of Divinity degree from the Maryknoll School of Theology in 1978, he was ordained for the missionary priesthood. Since 1975 he has served as a Maryknoll missionary in Peru among the Aymara people of the southern Andes. He is at present a Ph.D. candidate in the area of Religion and Society at the Graduate Theological Union in Berkeley, California.

LUIS MALDONADO was born in Madrid in 1930, and ordained priest in 1954. He studied philosophy in the Universities of Comillas and Freiburg, and theology in Salamanca and Innsbruck, where he gained his doctorate under

K. Rahner. He is Professor in the Pontifical University of Salamanca, and Principal of the Instituto Superior de Pastoral in the same University. His publications include: *La nueva secularidad* (1968); *La secularización de la liturgia* (1970); *La violencia de lo sagrado* (1974); *Religiosidad popular. Nostalgia de lo mágico* (1976); *Génesis del Catolicismo popular* (1979); *Introducción a la Religiosidad popular* (1985).

CRISTIAN PARKER was born in Santiago Chile in 1953. He studied sociology at the Catholic University of Chile (1972-76) and development in the ILADES (Latin American Institute of Social Teaching and Study) (1977-78). In 1985 he defended his doctoral thesis in sociology at the University of Louvain (Belgium). He was formerly national leader of the Catholic University graduates. At present he is affiliated to MIIC-Pax Romana. He has worked for many years in popular areas and collaborated in popular pastoral care. He was a member of Eq. de Invest. de la Zona Oeste, Archdiocese of Santiago, and Executive Secretary of the Deputation of Laity to the Chile Episcopal Conference until 1981. He has published many articles on sociology and pastoral matters.

WLADYSLAW PIWOWARSKI was born in 1929 at Mokrzyska, near Brzesko, Poland. He studied philosophy and theology at the Tarnów theological institute and at the Hosianum at Olsztyn (Allenstein), and studied the social sciences at the Catholic University of Lublin from 1949 to 1958. In 1959 he became assistant for the sociology of religion at Lublin and in 1961 gained his doctorate of philosophy. From 1961 to 1967 he taught the sociology of religion at Lublin and in 1967 gained his *Habilitation* in that field. Since 1970 he has been professor of the sociology of religion at Lublin, and in 1976/77 he was senior research fellow at the Divinity School, Yale. Among his publications are a study of religious practice in the diocese of Ermland (Warmia) (*Praktyki religijne diecezji warmińskiej. Studium socjograficzne* 1969), a study of rural religion under the influence of urbanisation (*Religijność wiejska w warunkach urbanizacji* 1971), and a study of urban religion in industrial areas (*Religijność miejska w rejonie uprzemyslowionym* 1977).

ROSEMARY RUETHER is the Georgia Harkness Professor of Applied Theology at the Garrett-Evangelical Theological Seminary in Evanston, Illinois, U.S.A. She is the author of numerous books and articles on feminist and liberation theology, among them *Sexism and God-Talk: Toward a Feminist Theology* (1983) and *Womanguides: Texts for Feminist Theology* (1985). She has completed a manuscript on feminist liturgical communities

(*Women-Church: The Theology and Practice of Feminist Liturgical Communities*) to be published by Harper and Row in the summer of 1986. Other books on Christian, Jewish and pagan feminist liturgical practice are: Linda Clark *et al, Image Breaking; Image Making: A Handbook for Creative Worship for Women in the Christian Tradition* (1980); Susannah Heschel *On Being a Jewish Feminist* (1983); *The Spiral Dance: The Rebirth of the Ancient Religion of the Goddess* (1979).

GIUSEPPE RUGGIERI teaches fundamental theology at the Theological Studium of St Paul in Catania. He is a member of the board of Editorial Directors of *Concilium* and editor of the Bologna Review *Cristianesimo nella Storia.* His published works include *La compagnia della fede. Linee di teologia fondamentale* (Turin, 1980).

SIDBE SEMPORÉ, OP., was born in 1938 in Ouagadougou (Burkina-Faso). He did his theological studies in France, Austria, Israel and Switzerland. He gained the diploma of the Ecole Biblique in Jerusalem. He teaches and conducts theological and biblical research in Benin, Nigeria and the Ivory Coast. He has published various articles and studies on religious life, Afro-Christian churches etc.

PAULO SUESS was born in Cologne in 1938, and ordained in 1964. He studied at Munich, Louvain and Munster, where he obtained his doctorate in theology. After eight years pastoral work in Amazonia, he was appointed lecturer in theology at Manaus, from 1977–79, when he also became secretary of the Council for Mission to the Indians. He is on the editorial board of the review *Porantim*, which works for the Indian cause, and has published *Volkskatholicismus in Brasilien* (1978), *Do grito à cancão* (1983) and *Cálice e cuia* (1985).

HERMANN VORLÄNDER was born in 1942, and studied theology in Bethel, Hamburg, Heidelburg and Erlangen. He is Director of the Theological Examinations Board for the Evangelical Lutheran Church of Bavaria and lectures in Old Testament at the Munich department of the Augustana College. His publications include *Mein Gott. Die Vorstellungen vom persönlichen Gott im Alten Orient und im Alten Testament* (1975); 'Die Entstehungszeit des jehowistischen Geschichtswerkes' (Frankfurt 1978) *Europäische Hochschulschriften XXIII*, 109; 'Der Monotheismus als Antwort auf die Krise des Exils' in *Der einzige Gott. Die Geburt des biblischen Monotheismus* ed. Bernhard Lang (1981) 84–113.

CONCILIUM

CONCILIUM

CONCILIUM 1985

*All back issues are still in print: available from bookshops (price £3.95)
or direct from the publisher (£4.45/US$7.70/Can$8.70 including postage
and packing).*

**T. & T. CLARK LTD, 59 GEORGE STREET,
EDINBURGH EH2 2LQ, SCOTLAND**